Are We Having Fun Yet?

Are We Having

FUN Yet?

The 16
Secrets of
Happy Parenting

Kay Willis and
Maryann Bucknum Brinley

WARNER BOOKS

A Time Warner Company

Warner Books, Inc., 1271 Avenue of the Americas, New York, NY 10020

W A Time Warner Company

First Printing: May 1997
10 9 8 7 6 5 4 3 2 1

Library of Congress Cataloging-in-Publication Data

Willis, Kay.
Are we having fun yet? : the 16 secrets of happy parenting /
Kay Willis and Maryann Bucknum Brinley.
p. cm.
ISBN 0–446–52043–8
1. Parenting. 2. Motherhood. 3. Mothers—Psychology. 4. Happiness.
I. Brinley, Maryann Bucknum. II. Title.
HQ755.8.W536 1997
649'.1—dc20 96–43904

Mothers Matter
is the direct result of the beautiful and joyful
example set by my mother,

ELLEN BURNS RUBACKY,

who SHARED *with me*
her positive outlook,

ENCOURAGED *in me*
a true sense of self-worth,

and always helped me to
ENJOY *my profession.*

[This simple dedication was displayed on the walls of the first Mothers Center,
established by Kay Willis in Rutherford, New Jersey, in March of 1978.]

Acknowledgments

To Mom, my constant inspiration and help.

To Bub, whose perfect love made my life a joy.

To my very own board of directors—JoEllen, Kim, Patty, Maureen, Fran, Jeane, Ben, Tim, Jerry and Dan—whose very being makes my heart soar.

To my original and ongoing support group of mothers— Theresa, Grace, Pat, Marge, Ellen and Marilyn. And, finally, special thanks to Alexandra Urdang at Warner Books.

—*Kay Willis*

Where would I be without the outrageously wise and wonderful support of family and friends? Thank you, thank you, to Bob, Zach and Maggie; all my supporters in the Bucknum and Brinley clans; my agent, Agnes Birnbaum; my friend Sue Gleason; the marvelous team of editors at Warner Books, led by my editor, Joann Davis; and especially my mother, Rita Leonard Bucknum, whose quiet yet powerful presence in my life showed me how to reach for parenting wisdom.

—*Maryann Bucknum Brinley*

Contents

Happy Parents . . .

Happy Parents . . .

Before We Begin . . .

Let me tell you about my friend Kay Willis. I've known her for more than a decade. If I do my job right, you will soon know her as well as I do. This is important. Why? Because she has a philosophy about parenting that could truly revolutionize the way you live your life—not to mention how much happier you may become.

Twenty years ago, Kay had a remarkably simple and yet simply great idea: Mothers need to share their secrets in order to increase their skills, confidence and enjoyment as parents. That's when this Rutherford, New Jersey, mother of ten founded Mothers Matter, an educational and support program that has helped thousands of mothers in hundreds of communities.

"Motherhood is like a secret society," Kay often tells me. "You don't really find out all about it until after you've been initiated." Sure, there are pages and pages of advice written by well-meaning experts, but so much of what we experience as parents still happens in what Kay calls "a conspiracy of silence." What's more, under the weight of all these words of wisdom, many parents are having an absolutely terrible time raising their children.

As if all the classic challenges of raising children aren't enough, contemporary mothers must also grapple with trendy new pressures, as well as the old GUILT with a capital G.

Guilt is a waste of time.

The mothers who sign up for Kay's groups bring their tears, their trials and their triumphs to a series of five two-hour sessions.

You'll meet some of them in the pages that follow. "You are the real professionals in parenting," Kay tells them. She's very convincing. Because such words come from Kay—one of the most dynamic, funny and wise women you will ever know—they believe her and in themselves.

Mothers Matter reaches fathers as well as mothers because one of the sessions—number five, in fact—is devoted entirely to dads. Kay also offers special programs for new mothers, single parents, full-time earning-money mothers, parents of adolescents and even grandparents.

Kay has appeared on *Oprah, Good Morning America, The Today Show, The CBS Morning Show, The Home Show, CNN* and *The Joan Rivers Show.* Reports on her work have appeared in many consumer magazines and major newspapers, including the *New York Times, Washington Post, USA Today, Christian Science Monitor, Record* and *Chicago Tribune.*

I've been a professional editor and writer for more than twenty years. I write magazine articles, books, newsletters and pamphlets from a home office on my third floor now. I'm also happily married to Bob Brinley and the mother of two adolescents, Zach and Maggie. Through the years, writing and editing for *Ladies' Home Journal, McCall's, Woman's Day, Health* and *Good Housekeeping,* I would turn to Kay Willis often for both professional and personal advice and counsel. When I sat in a director's chair at the *Good Housekeeping* Infants and Childrens Laboratory, Kay was always the person with the sanest answers.

She's funny. She's on your side. And she rarely ever takes "No" when the answer ought to be "Yes." Here's a true story you will enjoy: I was a senior editor at *McCall's* magazine creating a monthly column called "The Mothers' Page." A call came in from Fisher-Price Toys. The representative wondered if I would be interested in a ten-city tour to promote a new toy for the Christmas season. "Not on your life," I told her. My children were younger then, and my job was already demanding enough. I just couldn't imagine being able to drop everything and go anywhere, especially during the fall weeks leading up to the holiday season. Santa Claus could never come to town if I left.

"I can't do it, but I have the perfect person for you," I told the woman hired by Fisher-Price to find a spokesperson. "You really have to meet my friend Kay Willis."

"Who is she? What makes you think she's right for this job? Is she an expert on children? On toys? A psychologist? A psychiatrist? A well-known author?"

"Well, she has ten children," I replied.

"Are you kidding?" she asked.

"No."

"Has she written anything?"

"No."

"Is she a magazine editor?"

"No."

"What makes her an expert?"

"Experience," I wanted to answer, but I didn't. I persisted and told her that Kay would be perfect. I explained how she had founded a support group for moms called Mothers Matter, but my contact still didn't want to hear another word about Kay.

I insisted that they speak with her, and the rep finally agreed, just as a courtesy to me. It turned out that their big toy for that particular season was going to be a camera for preschoolers. A camera? Yes, a camera for little children. Kay was undaunted. She wanted to become a spokesperson, yet a phone interview was all that Fisher-Price would grant to her. She was curtly and politely put off. During the conversation, however, Kay learned that the company had decided to look for a camera expert to send across the United States for television and radio interviews. A camera expert? To engage preschoolers and their moms and dads? Yes! She couldn't believe her good fortune. With this news, she put a dollar in an envelope along with a note to her interviewer. "I'll bet you a dollar that I can sell more toy cameras than your camera expert—unless that expert is a mother, too."

Two days later, the company called. "We want to see you."

At Kay's meeting with the president of Fisher-Price in upstate New York, her good humor caught him off guard. He asked Kay what made her think she knew anything about his company, and she quickly replied, "Why, I spend so much money on toys annually that I've been putting Fisher-Price on my tax return for years." He laughed, and she soon got the job.

Kay went on to become one of the most successful spokespersons the company ever hired. She considered the experience a great opportunity to not only talk about toys but share her message with parents in twenty-two cities. She also got to ride in a limousine. So used to traveling in a station wagon with her children, she found it luxurious to sit in the back of a limo alone. "Drive up and down the street," she told the driver assigned to pick her up one morning. She wanted to relish the feeling. She wanted the world—of Rutherford, at least—to see how far she had come. She was having fun.

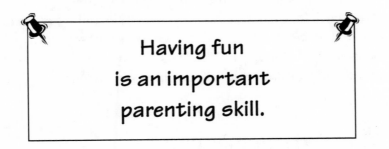

**Having fun
is an important
parenting skill.**

Kay's message is always delivered guilt-free. "I focus on mothers' needs," she explains. "Having fun is a very important parenting skill, but if you are overcommitted and exhausted, you aren't very much fun to be around."

Kay makes startling statements that ring true in mothers' ears: "You are the most important gift you will ever give your children. Too few of us act on this knowledge. You may strive to give your kids the best possible education, special lessons and great opportunities, but all these should be *supplements*, not *substitutes* for you."

Happy Parents = Successful Kids

"Success means different things to different people," Kay says. "Some parents might want to point to SAT scores, for instance. To me, however, success means raising a contented human being—someone who contributes to a better society and enjoys being in the same room with me." How can anyone argue with such wisdom? Much of the Mothers Matter program is philosophically simple, yet its wisdom will boggle your mind.

"All of my ten children have gone to college and some have graduate degrees, but one of my greatest successes is the fact that they can still be in the same room together as a family without a fight breaking out. They enjoy each other's company as well as mine. When you fail at childraising, you hurt yourself as well as your child. When you succeed, the payoff is extraordinarily rewarding and life-lasting."

What Do Happy Parents Like Kay Willis Know That You Need to Know Now?

There are sixteen secrets in our "collage" of lessons; each is the basis of its own chapter in the following pages. You'll also discover that in this book other voices play key roles. I introduce Kay's ideas and then put the book into Kay's own words. Like a good recipe, which almost always has a variety of ingredients, other people's thoughts, other mothers' voices and dads' words, are sprinkled throughout.

For the past two decades, Kay has been speaking, writing, traveling and making notes about parents. Her experience as the mother of ten successful children and the messages from her own mother are undoubtedly the backbone of this book. However, we could not have written it without the wise words of all the mothers who shared what matters.

About Maryann

My co-author, Maryann, is always more than generous in her descriptions of me. However, I think you need to know more about her. She is an absolutely wonderful package of spirited personality, good humor and recognized abilities as a writer and editor. My husband would have described her as adorable and, if it didn't seem to diminish her talents somewhat, I would too. She is a contented wife and happy mother. She does it all well. You should see her make a computer do tricks. Is there a downside to this woman? Yep. She keeps a large, simply beautiful house perfectly. I am really proud of myself for sticking with this relationship and getting to love her—despite the threat she poses to my ego. I thoroughly enjoy being with her and I'm constantly learning from her. There is no conspiracy of silence between us. In fact, we have shared some dark and depressing moments with each other. I have learned that she is not perfect, but don't tell anyone that because she is darn close to it.

How to Enjoy This Book

Think of a conversation as you begin.

Picture yourself seated across from Kay . . . at my kitchen table . . . in my third-floor office . . . in any one of the thousands of Mothers Matter sessions she has offered in the past twenty years . . . or seated in an audience as she lectures.

Envision a scrapbook—of voices, quotes, ideas and reminders you'll want to post on your refrigerator.

Don't start at the beginning and race through to the end.

Do flip through the pages. You can start and stop anywhere you choose.

Don't read while standing up. (Put your feet up, in fact.)

Do laugh out loud at anything that strikes you as funny.

Remember to have fun (an important part of the learning process).

Add your own best and worst moments of parenting wherever and whenever you can.

Share with us. (Our address is on the last page.)

Are We Having Fun Yet?

"Secrets, Kay," I say, "mothers want to know your secrets. How did you do it? What does it take to raise happy, healthy children? So many of my friends who are parents are worried, anxious, wondering if what they are doing is right and wishing that life wasn't so rushed."

It's January 1995, and Kay Willis is finally sitting down to work on a book—a book about her parenting secrets. We've been talking about this project for a decade. She's been writing one in her mind's eye for two decades. We face each other across my kitchen table. She has brought fat-free muffins. I drink coffee; she drinks tea. Calm—as ever—this soon-to-be sixty-five-year-old mother of ten and grandmother of ten almost always has a smile in her voice. She laughs easily and delivers one-liners with aplomb. Her wisdom is uncanny and always obviously true. Mothers like myself hang on her words, waiting to laugh and to learn from her experience.

This is a woman who has raised ten healthy, happy children. They all went to college. They still love her. She still loves them. So what comes first on her list of essentials?

1. Happy Parents . . .
Enjoy Parenting—
They Don't Endure It

Eavesdrop on busy parents chatting and commiserating with one another and too often you'll hear:

- ➤ "I can't wait until she is out of diapers."
- ➤ "It'll be great when he can finally walk."
- ➤ "I can't wait for her to start school."
- ➤ "I can't wait for summer vacation."
- ➤ "I can't wait for vacation to be over."
- ➤ "I can't wait for him to get his driver's license."

These parents are merely *enduring* their roles, not *enjoying* them.

If you're not enjoying the stage your child is in, chances are you will not enjoy the next stage either. **Enjoyment is a**

key element in anything you do. When you enjoy what you are doing, no matter what it is—even something you've decided you simply "must do" or "have to do"—the task becomes easier and more rewarding.

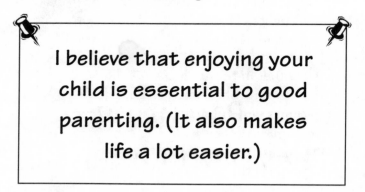

> I believe that enjoying your child is essential to good parenting. (It also makes life a lot easier.)

Each stage of parenting brings with it new joys as well as new problems. (I like to call them challenges.) The "Guess what she did today" kind of experiences can make you want to cry or laugh out loud, from the terrible twos right through to the terrifying teens.

After a really tough day—or two or three—it's easy to fall into the trap of wishing away your children's childhood. We all do this sometimes.

"To love what you do and to feel that it matters—how could anything be more fun?"

—Washington Post *editor* Katharine Graham

➤ If you are constantly anticipating a rosier future, a time when life with your kids will become better than ever, you run the risk of missing the joys of today.

➤ You can't count your blessings if you can't see them.

➤ Enjoying your children's development should become second nature to you.

➤ Change your focus so you can stop enduring and start enjoying what surely ought to be one of your life's most glorious adventures: parenting.

I pass a mother in the grocery store during baseball season. She laments that the afternoon games are ruining her routine. No time to prepare dinner. Everyone eating at different times. Evenings are a disaster. Hours and hours at the side of the ball field, she complains.

Later that day, my plumber pines for the days when his boys were young and he was able to stand at the side of the same baseball field to watch them play and cheer with the other parents. "Those were the days," he admits. "Those were the days."

You can't discover the best parts of each and every age—or experience any new joys —if you aren't in good shape emotionally as well as physically.

➤ Are you overtired?

➤ Are you overworked? (Underpaid is a given.)

➤ Are you in overload?

➤ **Are you having any fun yet?**

> "**When mine were little, I could never find the scissors, a pencil, a rubber band or the tape when I needed them. Now that my children are grown, I am so well organized. I can find almost anything when I need it—but so what? There's not a laugh or a hug to be had. I know I didn't think so then, but they grow up so fast. It is all over so quickly.**"
>
> *—a grandmother*

> Do you have at least two hours a week, every week, to call your own? (Not at nap time and not at 11 P.M., but time when someone else is responsible for your child.)

In the first of five Mothers Matter sessions, moms share their feelings about the best and worst moments of parenting. I ask the very same questions I'm asking you now. The most important question is: Do you have two hours a week for yourself, to do something you really enjoy?

" **Happiness depends upon ourselves.** "

—*Aristotle*

Invariably the group response is a low-level mumble. Very few nod yes.

> "I can't imagine a whole two hours to myself."

> "No, just when I have my hand up the chicken, someone needs me."

> "I know I don't treat myself well."

The second question is: If you do get two hours, how do you spend this time? And if you don't, what would you like to do if you could grab two hours just for yourself?

> "I can't even remember what I love to do."

> "I'd go grocery shopping ALONE!"

> "I'd exercise."

> "I'd read."

> "I'd nap."

> "I'd like to be in my own house alone."

➤ "I'd go OUT, O-U-T."

➤ "I'd read today's paper, today."

➤ "I'd talk to another adult."

"Time to be by myself . . . time to be with myself."

—*Candice Bergen*

From the thousands of answers I've heard in the past twenty years, my personal favorite is: "I'd shave both my legs on the same day." Audience after audience of parents howls at this woman's wish. She's funny, of course, but her plight isn't.

Answer these three good questions:

➤ Do you take two hours a week to do something you love?

➤ What would you do if you could?

➤ What do you consider fun?

(If you can't think of anything, then you really need this time off.)

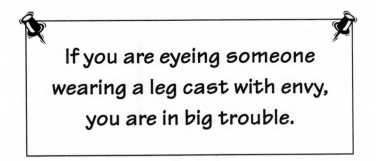

If you are eyeing someone wearing a leg cast with envy, you are in big trouble.

Sit down. Do it now. Let's take a look at your day. Whether you're a full-time at-home mom, a part-time working mom or a full-time earning-money mom, you probably have a sixteen-hour day. Do your math. This is your work week if you are an average mother:

> **"They asked me what I did all day. I said, 'Nothing,' and they believed me."**
>
> —*Mother of four*

7 days × 16 hours a day = 112 hours a week!

And you don't have even two hours a week for yourself. I truly believe that having fun is a parenting skill. Like laughter, it is one of life's best medicines, but too often it is overlooked by busy mothers and fathers.

Just how much fun are you to be around?

How does your child perceive you?

➤ The director?

➤ The organizer?

➤ The cleaner?

➤ The cook?

➤ The bottlewasher?

➤ The disciplinarian?

➤ The tutor?

➤ The grammarian?

➤ The shopper?

➤ How about the postponer?

Are you a postponer?

Check yourself. Does this sound like you?

➢ Not now . . .

➢ If Mommy gets through . . .

➢ When we get finished . . .

➢ We'll see . . .

➢ Maybe later . . .

➢ Just a minute . . .

➢ Not today . . .

➢ After dinner . . .

➢ I'll be with you in a second . . .

➢ If we get done . . .

➢ After your homework . . .

Then (maybe) we can have some fun.

Look at your parenting day as a pie with just so many pieces. One for cleaning (the kids, the house, the laundry), one for cooking, one for shopping (for food, clothes, home essentials), one for transportation, one for medical checkups, one for children's social development (homework, discipline, school involvements like the bake sales, fund-raisers and teacher conferences), perhaps a big piece for working and of course, one for phone time.

> **The most wasted day of all is that on which we have not laughed.**
> —Sebastien Chamfort

➢ How often is there a slice—even just a sliver—for fun time?

➢ Are you just too hurried?

➢ Are you just too tired to laugh?

➢ Do you even have any time left to be nice or to do something nice for somebody?

True Stories

We Don't Have Time to Be Nice, Mr. Brown

One of the very busy working mothers in my sessions had no idea of the impact rushing had taken on her family life until one morning. Allison, her preschooler, was certainly along for the rush. It was early. This mom was late. Older kids had raced out the door to waiting school buses. The kitchen was a mess. Beds were unmade. Where were the shoes? What about a load of laundry? this mother wondered. Her mind was a whirl. Could she start the washing machine now? Throw the clothes into the dryer that evening?

> **" It is not how much we have, but how much we enjoy what we have that makes happiness. "**
> —*Charles H. Spurgem*

Allison's mom was in the kind of race full-time employed moms know only too well. She had to get organized, get ready, get out that door to drop her youngest at daycare and catch the train for work. "We don't have time for that," this mom kept telling little Allison. "We don't have time right now, Allison. We'll do it later. We just don't have time to stop now."

In our Mothers Matter session later, she admitted that she was literally dragging Allison by the arm down the front walk when her elderly neighbor spotted them. Mr. Brown was eighty-something. Mr. Brown loved little Allison and looked forward to seeing her. She was a little light in his quiet life—a bright spot in his empty day. He started to wave hello, to begin a conversation that might only last a moment. "Hi there, Allison," he said. "We don't have time to be nice today, Mr. Brown," Allison replied sweetly.

"Allison, how could you?" the mother said, turning to her daughter in startled recognition. "Why, Mr. Brown, that's not exactly what she meant," she continued, trying to dig herself out. But it was exactly what this mom had been saying: No time to be nice.

Are You (Always) on Maintenance Duty?

I remember a dad in one of my sessions. "Kay," he said, "when I'm at work, I'm a professional person." (He was a Ph.D.) "But when I get home, I'm nothing but a maintenance man. All my wife and I ever do is get everybody and everything cleaned up so we can get ready for the next round of cleanup. We are not really living a good life at home, we are just maintaining the status quo."

Question: Do you really believe you can get it all done, every day?

Answer: Of course you can't.

Question: Do you really believe you need to get it all done, every day?

Answer: Of course you don't.

> ➤ Slow down so you can see better.

> ➤ Save time to do nothing.

> ➤ Create a fun reserve and draw on it regularly. If parenting experts suddenly pronounced that the way to raise brighter, happier, healthier, more successful children was to have unstructured, silly, lighthearted fun

" A mother is someone who looks forward to getting a cavity filled so she can sit quietly in one place. "

—*Beth Mende Conny,*
**A Mother Is
Someone Who**

daily, then you would find a way to fit it into your life. **Do it. Now.**

➤ Too busy with other obligations? Then simplify or eliminate, eliminate, eliminate chores. We often talk of the burden and responsibility of parenting in such negative terms. We believe that our jobs as mothers and fathers are impossibly difficult, and then we act upon those beliefs. What kind of message does this send to the kids in your life?

> " **I do so many disconnected things at the same time.** "
>
> —*Stay-at-home mother of a three-month-old, a three-year-old and a thirteen-year-old*

➤ Change your approach.

➤ Let the laundry wait.

➤ Forget the cereal on the kitchen floor.

➤ Get down on your children's level and play. (It's hard to be serious when you are on the floor.)

➤ Join the What the Hell Club, where fun is more important than a completed to-do list.

Each December, as the busy-ness of the holiday season began, my mother often warned me to slow down. "Things are getting out of control here," she would say. "If you don't start taking better care of yourself, everyone will get sick and you'll tell me that there is a 'bug' going around. There isn't any virus around here. The virus is you."

Problem: How do you put fun into your family's life?

It starts with you. Are you having any fun yet? When was the last time you had a simply marvelous time? What would you like to do for fun this week? Can you recall when you had two hours *all* to yourself?

Make it happen. Get a sitter. Trade childcare times with your husband, your neighbor or another mother.

Solution: Two moms in one of our sessions had already started taking turns minding each other's children, but they didn't like going out alone. They found two more moms. The four now rotate. Two stay with all the kids—more fun for the sitters—and the other two go out.

> **" When you finally allow yourself to trust joy and embrace it, you will find that you dance with everything. "**
>
> —*Emmanuel*

Even in a financial pinch, somehow, some of you find ways to pay for music lessons, soccer camps, adorable T-shirts and even prescriptions. Think of your two hours as a preventive mental health investment. The dividends are family benefits. You are not being selfish. You are practicing good parenting.

This week, block out two solid hours on your calendar and write **Me** in the space. Go for it. Enjoy!

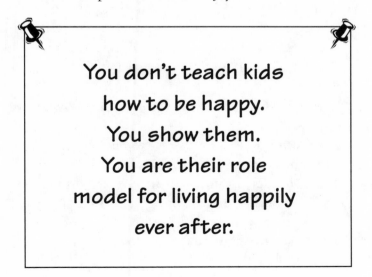

You don't teach kids how to be happy. You show them. You are their role model for living happily ever after.

Kay Remembers . . .

 # I Always Wanted to Be a Mother

I am one of five children. I grew up in Passaic, New Jersey, where my father was both a doctor and a lawyer. We were raised to have a great respect for education. My mother, whom I thoroughly enjoyed, never finished high school, but was a wise woman and very funny. Both my parents made me feel very loved and very capable—just as intellectually capable as my three older brothers. Being a woman would never hold me back. All of my siblings are professionals, but for as long as I can remember, I always wanted to be a mother.

When I was in kindergarten, the principal of my school, Miss Haggerty, called me out of class because members of the local Board of Education were touring the school and she wanted them to meet a youngster with great educational ambition. Out of class I marched, where I stood in front of the principal and her visiting dignitaries.

"Kay, tell our guests what you want to be when you grow up," she said.

"Oh, I want to be a mother," I replied politely. At age five, I had no concept at all about what it took to become a mother. (In fact, I remember hearing at seven about a little girl in South America who gave birth at age nine. I believed she was the luckiest soul in the world. It could happen, I used to tell myself; I'll keep praying.)

Miss Haggerty looked quite disturbed. Clearly, this wasn't the answer she was going for. She paused and then rephrased her question. "Kay, dear, what would you like to be before you become a mother?"

"Oh, I want to be a mother as soon as possible," I said earnestly.

Miss Haggerty and I stayed in touch over the years. On the birth of my first child, I received a note of congratulations from her. "At last," she wrote. "You did it."

Years later, after her retirement, she traveled a lot and would send me little treasures occasionally from around the world: gifts for my babies—booties, lace from Belgium. However, the most memorable gift from Miss Haggerty arrived after her death. More than thirty years had passed since that memorable encounter in the school hallway. I had several children by then. I received a phone call from a relative, telling me that Miss Haggerty had died and that an unlabeled gift-wrapped package had been left in her apartment. When the Haggerty family opened it, they discovered a beautiful antique glass with the word "Mother" etched inside a wreath.

"There was no doubt about it. We knew this glass was for you, Kay."

I will always treasure it. My "mother" glass runneth over.

I live across the street from a nursery school. Mothers and babysitters arrive and depart daily with infants, toddlers and preschoolers. Waiting for Kay to arrive one sunny Friday morning, I watch a mother peek into her carriage and then laugh with her baby. Her three-year-old has already been handed over to the waiting teacher on the doorstep of the school. Baby and mom are alone together. They giggle. They laugh. Then they head down the street toward town.

Could this simple act—a contented adult and child laughing together—be as important as Kay Willis tells me it is? I smile at the simplicity. The happy pair makes me happy, too. Funny how good moods are contagious. Kay's car pulls up. She parks and walks toward my door. I'm still seated on the step. "Look," I say, pointing to the mother and baby now two doors down. "There goes a parent who is really enjoying her kids."

"She understands the Rs," Kay says.

2. Happy Parents . . .
Refuel, Restore, Renew

Think back to the last time you were on an airplane waiting to take off. Do you remember those emergency instructions? "In the event of a problem with the air pressure in the plane's cabin, an oxygen mask will drop down from an overhead compartment." The stewardess always demonstrates exactly how to attach the mask and if you are flying with an infant or young child, however, she will add, "Put the mask on yourself first. Take care of yourself first. Then you will be better able to care for your child."

> **"There is no such thing as a nonworking mother."**
> —*Anonymous*

Parenting reminds me of those emergency flying instructions. Catch your breath first. Moms, especially, are great at giving, giving, giving—rarely stopping to care for themselves.

Refuel. Restore. Renew.

These are just three of the Rs of healthy parenting. There's also rest, revive (absolutely essential), relax, rejuvenate, reenter—and how about refresh?

Nobody Tells You What Parenting Is Really Going to Be Like

In the first session of any Mothers Matter seminar, I urge moms to recognize their own needs and to respond to them.

> **" I'd like to spend an hour in a gourmet deli eating all the free samples. "**
>
> —*Manhattan mother*

Most women know what is missing from their lives, but far too few act on filling the void. Brand-new mothers desperately need rest, confidence, self-esteem and adult conversation. In too many cases, exhaustion, tears, a sense of inadequacy, resentment and isolation fill their days. Guilt is in a category all by itself. These feelings keep recurring for mothers. I remember how hard it was with my first baby. Exhausted and teary, I was definitely not loving my role as a new mommy. I felt so inadequate and so guilty. **Nobody had told me what it was really going to be like.**

Your physical need for rest is paramount. Taking time to refuel and renew yourself ought to become automatic for mothers. If it doesn't, depression may.

The message sounds so simple—and I know I repeat it often—but mothers look askance at me when I insist that the benefits are real. They groan, they moan and they offer a host of excuses for why time off is truly impossible.

➤ "I would never leave my baby with someone other than family."

➤ "I'm too tired to go out."

➤ "There are no sitters out where I live."

➤ "I can't afford a sitter."

➤ "My husband leaves at 6:00 A.M. and doesn't come home until 8:00 P.M."

➤ "We have no family living near us."

➤ "I am away too long each day as it is."

> " [A] woman's life today [1955] is tending more and more toward the state William James describes so well in the German word *Zerrissenheit*— torn-to-pieces-hood."
>
> —*Anne Morrow Lindbergh,* **Gift from the Sea**

A saying I once heard in a business management course goes like this: "Argue for your limitations and they are yours." I have met too many moms who limit themselves, vehemently protesting that there is no such thing as time off for a good mother. To be good, in fact, means to sacrifice every waking moment to your family. What they don't realize as they constantly give of themselves— never replenishing their own emotional resources—is that no child deserves a martyr for a mother.

➤ "I worry about asking for help," mothers protest.

➤ "My family will think I'm selfish if I go off alone," some insist.

➤ "I've always done everything for them, I'm worried about what they will think if I try to stop now," others admit.

> # Are you serving your
> # family leftover you?

Think and remember:

> ➤ You are not a complainer, a slacker or selfish when you seek relief from a satisfying yet grueling schedule.

> ➤ Time off from a demanding routine becomes the equivalent of money in your emotional bank account. These are funds you will almost certainly borrow on a day when life lets you down and feeling overwhelmed or trapped can make you miserable.

> ➤ A refueled, restored, renewed mother can get through the day-to-day drudgery and unpleasant surprises. She can laugh at herself and *with* her child. Can you?

True Stories

Six Girls in Seven Years!

I do remember what it is to feel tired and trapped. Our daughter JoEllen was born in April 1951, exactly nine months and twenty-three days after our wedding. Kim arrived in August 1952. Patty came in December 1953. Then we skipped a year, and Maureen was born in May 1955. I gave birth to Fran in October 1956, and Jeane came in February 1958. That was six girls in seven years, in case you lost count.

"Are you trying for a boy?" was the comment I'd hear often. We weren't. My husband, Bub, used to say, "God knows what would have happened if we tried!"

I was busy, yet I was young and enjoying my children, except for the bouts of morning sickness. I used to be so nauseous during my pregnancies that the girls and I would play a game we called EMERGENCY. When I yelled EMERGENCY, my little girls learned to stop whatever they were doing and sit very still so they wouldn't get into anything dangerous while I was indisposed. They'd wait until my nausea had passed. For the longest time, their concept of EMERGENCY was of someone getting sick to her stomach. An emergency vehicle would pass the house, and they'd say, "Oh look, Mom, an EMERGENCY."

"I'm so lonesome. My kids have been barred from the library and I've been banned from the supermarket when I'm with them."

—*Mother of three boys, all under age four*

I truly did ENJOY being the mother of ten children—not every minute, of course, but most of the time. I wasn't often overwhelmed, and frequently I was filled with joy. My enjoyment did not come from my being particularly gifted as a parent or because I was simply too stupid to understand the situation. It was quite clearly because of the help and support I got from my mother and my husband. Their insistence on at least three of the Rs being present in my life was a message that was repeated often. Together, they took very good care of me, always reminding me that I was incredibly important and that no one else could do what I was doing. (If you have no one else to take care of you, you must care for yourself.)

"You're got to realize," my mother would say, "that if anything happens to you, we've got to bring in a whole squad to replace you. It's better for you—and for me—if you get out at least once a week." (I think she was afraid that she would get all ten kids.) "It's good preventive medicine," she'd say. So she made sure I had every Thursday afternoon off. No matter how bad Monday, Tuesday or Wednesday was, I knew that on Thursday, I would get my chance to walk away and refuel, then reenter, restored.

> **" One of my hobbies?" she asks quietly, looking around at the group of fifteen other mothers in our circle. "Folding clothes. "**
>
> —*Mother of three with a great sense of humor*

My Thursday afternoons away were part of the fabric of our family life. Everyone expected me to be gone and I relished my time away. Your family will recognize the difference in you when you are recharged.

My mother was an extraordinarily wise woman. Many of my Mothers Matter messages, in fact, are my mother's messages to me. "You are not being fair to your children when you are so tired that your judgement is impaired. Even obvious solutions escape you when you are tired or burned out." How many of us have lashed out in anger at a child who simply was not the problem?

Although I know how concerned my mother was about our having so many children, she never attempted to interfere. Always a humorous woman, she did say that Dr. Reilly, our family doctor—and the man who delivered all ten of our children without ever sending a bill—might think we were making pigs of ourselves. His services were free, given to us as a professional courtesy, because both Bub's and my father were on staff at the hospital where he practiced.

When time off becomes a regular part of your life, your family is more apt to accept and support your need to refresh and refuel yourself.

When my mother heard the news of our first pregnancy, she congratulated Bub. He answered proudly, "It's a feather in a man's cap when he discovers he can conceive." Eight announcements later, my mother simply said, "Hi, Chief!"

Bub, a family nickname for Benedict Patrick Willis Jr., was an unbelievably thoughtful man, a true gentleman. He died in 1988 of cancer. Loving and caring, he was always more serious than I. No matter what shape I was in, he made me believe that I was just great. Always generous with his compliments, even in my ninth month of pregnancy, Bub would tell me I had beautiful eyes. He would do anything for me and our children. He was the parent who bathed our babies each night.

> " I had major surgery last summer. I thoroughly enjoyed it. "
>
> —*Overtired working mother of two*

Good thing, too, because most of the time I couldn't reach the tub. When the children were little, he lived by this rule: "I won't sit down until you can sit down." Sometimes his rule worked so well that I would put off doing a chore because he looked weary and needed to sit down more than I did. We didn't get everything done, but boy, did I feel loved. I always knew he loved me, but feeling loved is the ultimate.

Question: What happens if you can't get time off? If the sitter is sick? If your husband is delayed at work? Or if your kids aren't welcome at the daycare because they have the chicken pox?

Suggestion: Treat yourself. I remember being forced to stay home with sick kids while the rest of my family—brothers, sisters, cousins and kids—went off for a day of special celebration. My clan was in quarantine with some kind of communicable childhood disease, and I was so disappointed I wanted to cry. My mom made a suggestion: "Ignore those routine chores that wouldn't have been touched if you were out all day. Instead," she said, "do something you've been itching to tackle but have never found time for. Treat yourself in some small way."

> **" I need to learn to be less driven. "**
>
> —*Mother of two*

What did I do? I organized my photo album and had a grand time doing so. It was "play" for me, and I loved it. Many a day since then, I have relied on a "play day" to renew myself.

This is a test: When was the last time you took a bath?

When I ask an audience this question, very few hands go up. Most moms haven't had a bath in a long, long time. Mothers don't have time. They're lucky if they can take a two-minute shower some days.

Here's a tip: To calm restless preschoolers, put them in a warm tub about 4:30 P.M. and sit down to chat with them. Warm water has a very calming effect on young children. Follow this with a candlelight dinner for the whole family. Don't worry about the food. Order pizza. Or serve breakfast. It's the candles and quiet that will be important. Toddlers love to whisper in the semidarkness. Everyone will settle down.

Warm water can help you relax, too. No matter how late it is when you finally get ready to climb into bed, stop and take a warm bath. There is no guarantee that you will sleep any longer, but you will probably sleep sounder.

> **" There are days when I really lose my enthusiasm for this job. "**
>
> —*Working mother of an only son, age four*

True Stories

Play Days

In our house, "play days" arrived when Bub had to be away on business for more than two days. My theory was: If you can't leave 'em, join 'em—the kids, I mean.

The rules were simple enough. On the first day, there would be no dishes, no beds to make, no laundry (unless I was desperate), no chores, and only paper plates for meals, which never included vegetables. When "play days" first began, I had five and then six little girls to play with. Often it became "doll day." We would take all the dolls we could find, strip them, wash and iron their clothes, re-dress them and brush their hair. (This was a real treat for me, because when I was little, not very many dolls had "real" hair.) When the boys entered the scene, on "play days" we would often move furniture around so we could drape bedspreads over everything to make tents. On the second day, everyone would pitch in to help put the house back in shape for Daddy's arrival home.

These "play days" became so popular that when Bub announced that he had to go away, cheers could be heard from our peanut gallery. We had to modify this behavior. Nevertheless, a family tradition was begun. Recently, I called one of my daughters at her office and was told she would not be in that day but could be reached at her home. Concerned about her health, I called her apartment.

"There's nothing wrong, Mom," she explained. "I'm just having a 'play day.' "

Post these definitions on your refrigerator:

re fu el \ *re-fyu l* *vt: to provide with additional fuel vi: to take on additional fuel*

" Necessity may be the mother of invention, but play is certainly the father."

—Roger von Oech

re new \ *ri-n (y) u* \ *vt* 1: *to make new again;* re *also: to gain again as new* 2: *to make new spiritually: regenerate* 3: *to restore to existence: revive* 4: *to do again: repeat* 5: *to begin again: resume* 6: *to replace* 7: *to grant or obtain an extension of or on vi* 1: *to become new or as new* 2: *to begin again: resume* 3: *to make a renewal*

re store \ *ri-'sto ( )r, -'sto ( )r* \ *vt ()ME restoren, OF restorer, fr. L restaurare to renew, rebuild, alter. of in-*

staurare, to renew—more at store] 1. *to give back: return*
2: *to put or bring back into existence or use* 3: *to bring*
back to or put back into a former or original state: renew;
esp: reconstruct 4: *to put again in possession of some-*
thing < the king to the throne> syn see renew

True Stories

A Babysitter . . .
for Nothing?

Just before the birth of our sixth child, we moved to a big house
in Rutherford, New Jersey. Before that we had lived in a tiny,
two-bedroom, one-story home. The big house
worried my mother. She was concerned about
all the stairs I'd be climbing all day long. I was
thrilled that we finally had an upstairs with
bedrooms out of sight, but my mother worried
about all the extra work of keeping a big
house, and especially those steps.

"I have a gift for you, but it comes with
strings attached," she said. "I will pay for a
babysitter to come to you every day at 5 P.M."

"At 5 o'clock? What can I do at that hour?"
I asked.

"Nothing. That's the point. I don't want
you to do anything but rest, freshen up, put on some lipstick
and pull yourself together. I'll be happy to pay for that."

Jane Elin was only fourteen when she started working for

> "I have darling
> sayings on my
> refrigerator,
> but I'm usually
> screaming at
> my kids."
>
> —*Mother of two,*
> *working part-time*

me as our weekday-everyday sitter. She stayed with us until she was twenty-four and quit only when she got married. Through her high school years and even during college, she would arrive each evening at 5 to be with my kids. In the warm months, they would play outside. During the winter, she'd bathe them and put the little ones into pajamas so the after-dinner routine could be shortened. In the beginning, my six little girls couldn't believe their good fortune, that this bright, energetic, teenage girl actually came to play with them. Jane Elin was full of verve and pep at a point in my day when I was wiped out. My energy was gone at 5 P.M. She offered them a chance to escape from me. Sometimes I think we forget that when we wish to be away from our kids, they need to be away from us.

Where did I go? Not far. Sometimes I'd just walk across the street to spend an hour sitting on a stool in my friend Theresa's kitchen. Theresa always had one more child than I did underfoot. She gave birth to twelve kids. I stopped at number ten. She would never let me help her with dinner on those late afternoons in her kitchen. "Your mom expects you to be sitting down at this hour. I'm just so happy to get the chance to chat. Thank her for me too," she would insist. These visits, which still occur as often as Theresa and I can manage, formed the warmest and strongest bond of friendship for both of us—a relationship we have treasured for more than thirty-five years. (Thank God for Mom, Theresa and Jane Elin.)

You are much too important to be poorly cared for.

Learn from one of nature's earliest teachers: the breastfeeding mother. In order to nourish her infant, a woman who is breastfeeding must care for herself first. If she doesn't eat, drink or rest enough, she won't be able to feed the baby who is so utterly dependent upon her, and she has to stop, sit down or even lie down to nurse her infant. Clever Mother Nature!

WILLIS FAMILY SNAPSHOTS

Two things come to mind when I think of my mother and look at her funny side. The first is her amazing "pregnancy sandwiches." She used to make up the craziest food combinations! One that sticks out clearly was her bologna and relish on wheat toast. The second is how different she was from other mothers. While most moms try to keep kids' crayoning off walls, Mom actually had each of us paint a picture in the basement. Those "murals" stayed up for about twenty years.

I remember dressing alike until JoEllen was old enough to rebel against looking the same as her youngest sister. I remember the laundry tags Mom made up for us when we went to day camp. They read "Ima Willis," because it was easier than getting ten different sets.

We operated on the "extended family plan" on holidays because we had numerous cousins living in the area. What great big parties they were! Only as an adult have I come to realize just how unusual that was . . . and still is.

—Pat

**Parents make
the single most
important contribution
to a better society.
All mothers matter.**

Kay Remembers . . .

Four Boys in a Row

Big families were more common when I was having babies. Rutherford is a town of big houses, and we weren't the only large family in our neighborhood. All around us were families with five, six, seven or more children. Bub was one of five children, and so was I. We both wanted a large family. We were often asked why we didn't "go for twelve."

Jokingly, I used to respond that it was because dishes and donuts came in sets of twelve, and the two of us would have gone hungry. I really do believe that you should never take anyone seriously when they say they want twelve children—unless they already have eleven.

As you may recall, Jeane was our sixth daughter in a

row, born on February 12, 1958. As I left for the hospital that day, the girls wanted to know: If the new baby was a boy, could they call him Abe? I said no. There was no way our firstborn son would not be named Benedict Patrick Willis III.

And so it was that Ben, a whopping eleven pounds, three ounces, was born in March of 1960. Up to that point, I had given birth every sixteen months. Now we reached a two-year mark. I was getting older—I was thirty at the time —and slowing down, I guess. When the news of our new baby boy was heard, a sister-in-law sent us a telegram: "Vive la différence!" We were to discover how true that is.

Amidst all the celebrations about a boy, I was concerned about Ben's growing up as the only son among all our little girls. (My fears were confirmed about three years later, when he asked to go to the powder room.) However, he was always every inch a boy; the girls' baby carriage was even used as a wagon. Nevertheless, I worried. We wanted Ben to have a brother, so we deliberately decided to become pregnant again—which wasn't all that difficult for me. It was the first time my mother questioned my mental competency. To me, it was an act of faith. I kidded her and said, "C'mon, Mom, it's no trick for God to just go to the boy box."

> **"A healthy four letter word for mothers: Exit."**
> —*Author Nancy Samalin*

Her comments must have caused me to waver just a tiny bit. We had always had the older children pray with us every night, and whenever I was pregnant and safely beyond the three-month stage, we'd pray for a healthy new baby. During this eighth pregnancy, we asked, "Please God, send us a healthy new Timothy."

I never had any doubt that Timothy was on his way. He—yes, he!—arrived in December 1961, a bit late because he was due in November, just twenty-one months after Ben. I remember how much we loved all the boy stuff. We were on a roll. My theory was: No one ever told Picasso to stop. Thank God, we didn't. Our Jerry was born in January of 1964 and, last but not least, another eleven-pounder, our Danny, was born in July 1966.

> " **I'm just on my way out (out of my mind).** "
>
> —*Mother of three*

All of our children have their own birthday months, if you discount the fact that Timothy arrived late in Patty's birthday month of December. We have no birthdays in September, because that's back-to-school month and we had to buy everyone shoes. Our anniversary is in June, so there is something to celebrate every month of the year. You see, we knew what we were doing all along!

One night, when my mom and dad were coming for dinner, as they frequently did, I was in the kitchen getting ready to serve dessert. I had made a layer cake, and one of the children asked to put on the candles.

"It isn't anybody's birthday today, honey," I said.

He looked so disappointed that I couldn't say no. I took out the candles, trying to think of a reason for the celebration. Meanwhile, I let the children cover the whole cake with all the candles I could find. Candles were a staple in our house. With dozens of candles ablaze on the cake, I carried it into the dining room.

My father looked surprised. With a straight face, I told him that we were celebrating my ninetieth month of pregnancy.

He cried.

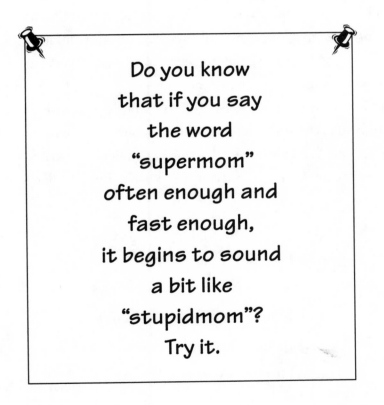

Do you know
that if you say
the word
"supermom"
often enough and
fast enough,
it begins to sound
a bit like
"stupidmom"?
Try it.

There are thirteen women seated in a circle in a church basement in northern New Jersey. Some are full-time earning-money moms. Some are full-time stay-at-home moms. (One has brought her baby and nurses as we speak.) Two are single. A few are employed part-time. All of us—even the reporter from Cable Network News (CNN) who is here to interview and film Kay for a Mother's Day television segment—share a dilemma: We truly undervalue our own importance as mothers.

Initially, I am surprised to think this. Then I change my mind.

> ➤ "I find it hard to ask for help—even when I am resentful and drowning in chores."
> ➤ "I make myself sick."
> ➤ "I know I should sit down . . . but I just can't."
> ➤ "In my other life, I could have called in sick."
> ➤ "I guess I just can't say no."

Kay is wearing a red silk tunic. She looks terrific. At one point, as the camera pans around the group and then back to her, she says, "We can all learn from big business."

3. Happy Parents...

Borrow from Big Business

If you were the chief executive officer (CEO) of a huge corporation, you would receive far more than a huge salary. Your compensation package would be filled with perks. One of the reasons the perks are so elaborate is because you are so valuable to the company. They want to keep you. They want to make sure you are happy—satisfied enough to perform for the good of the company. Ask successful executives, and they will admit that money alone is not their real motivation.

> **The hand that rocks the cradle is the hand that rules the world.**
> —*W. R. Wallace*

- ➤ "It isn't about money."
- ➤ "I love what I do."

➢ "I feel that I am making a real contribution."

➢ "I love the challenge."

CEOs are treated so generously—physically as well as financially—for at least three reasons: 1) so they will stay healthy, 2) so they will stay with the company, and 3) so they will produce the best results.

You are in the business of parenting. You are the CEO in your home. I borrow a lot of ideas from big business for my work with parents. Consider how it might pay you to emulate some of these practices:

> " **God could not be everywhere, so he created mothers.** "
>
> —*Jewish proverb*

➢ Coffee breaks

➢ Quitting time

➢ Vacations

➢ Personal days

➢ Courses and seminars

➢ Comp time

➢ Quarterly reports and,

➢ Expense accounts!

Let's start with the **coffee break**. In the introductory session I ask moms, "How many of you, who are at home, sit down every morning and have a coffee break?" (The operative words here, of course, are "sit down.") This eliminates carrying the mug upstairs to make beds. You won't be able to leave it on the dryer when you run to answer the phone, either.

Big businesses pay employees while they take coffee breaks. Even the checker at your local supermarket gets a break. Studies have shown that the employee who stops to take a break—and refuels—is not only more efficient at the end of the day but is also more productive. If you take coffee breaks, you will be more rational. You can't go nonstop all day.

Full-time earning-money moms tell me that they cherish their breaks at work. They use them to collect their thoughts and to make lists. On their days at home (which are never really days off for mothers), they've learned to take breaks as well.

Now let's consider **quitting time**. Nine to five is an impossible concept for parents. Yet Scarlett O'Hara may have been talking to mothers when she said, "After all, tomorrow is another day."

> " **For many years, I've been a consultant and guest lecturer at a nearby college for its master's degree program in Parent Education. Less than 50 percent of the candidates for this program are parents.** "
>
> —*Kay*

➤ Know when it's time to stop the chores and start to smell the pot roast.

➤ Put a limit on your output. Establish a true quitting time—hours before your bedtime—for yourself and your spouse.

➤ Close your "office" so you can spend some quantity time with your family—time to learn about one another's day, time to listen, time to laugh, time to exchange loving words.

Vacation time for a mother usually means that you simply relocate your workplace. After an intense period of planning and packing for the whole clan, your vacation may be little more than a change of scenery—minus a washing machine and dryer—where you continue to respond to your family's needs.

➤ Ever feel like you'd like to get away from it all?

➤ An overnight at a nearby hotel that offers special weekend rates AND a massage sound like a fantasy to you?

➤ Have a fund-raiser for yourself!

➤ Perhaps another mother would go along and split the cost of a hotel room. If their father can stay with the kids, you won't incur any babysitting costs. (I know of four moms who shared the price of a hotel room for their "sleepover.")

➤ When was the last time you laughed so hard your sides ached?

A good idea:

One young mom "borrowed" her grandmother's beach house for a weekend and invited every mother in the session. What a blast they had. Can you imagine catering to no one but yourself for just twenty-four hours? This kind of escape translates into time to RESTORE with a capital "R."

> " **My husband hands me his list of things to do every day.** "
>
> —*Tearful at-home mother of four*

Years ago, I discovered the tremendous rejuvenating power of time spent away from home and with another mother. When I still couldn't afford my own ice cream cone and just licked from the kids' dripping pops, my friend Marilyn, who now owns several craft shops, would take me along on buying and selling trips. In those first years, we would pack her van and exhibit her wares at craft shows. The lifting and hauling, setting up and taking down, and eating lunch in our booth never seemed like work. We would share very personal thoughts and laugh and laugh as we covered the miles. When you spend time with another mom, you don't have to cater to anyone else's needs. Nothing is a big deal. *He* doesn't get to pick the movie. No one grumbles if the restaurant was a poor choice. Today, Marilyn and I still go on buying trips for her shops. However, now we travel first class. The end result has remained the same: I reenter my life at home feeling relaxed and refueled.

> **" I used to joke that in terms of the business of running our family, I was in production and Bub was in sales. One mother remarked, 'Whew. He's quite a salesman.' "**
>
> —*Kay*

Working away from home?

➤ Plan to arrive home later than usual at least once a week.

➤ Stop at a store. Browse.

➤ Buy yourself flowers.

➤ Meet a friend for dinner. It's up to you to make it happen, and it might take some ingenuity to arrange. Yet you could be surprised by the ease of negotiating for the sitter to stay a bit longer or for someone else to take care of your "after-work" child-care ritual. You will bring home more joy and less stress if you stop to refuel. Treat your kids to a relaxed, more enjoyable you.

In many companies, employees are allotted a number of **personal days** to use at their discretion. Corporations recognize this practice as a worthwhile preventive mental health measure. You should, too.

When was the last time you had a day off, a personal day to spend on yourself? A day spent in bed with the flu does not

> " **By and large, mothers are the only workers who do not have regular time off. They are the great vacation-less class.** "
>
> —*Anne Morrow Lindbergh,* **Gift from theSea**

count! Many mothers never even think about a day off as a possibility. If you are working full-time away from home, you are even less likely to take a day.

➤ Why not trade days with another mother?

➤ Call someone you know who desperately needs time off and offer to take responsibility for her children for a day if she'll reciprocate and take yours on another occasion.

➤ Can't think of anyone willing to trade time? Please, please, ask someone for help, because you need to stay healthy emotionally as well as physically. Don't wait until you are sick (or just sick and tired). Make time to rejuvenate before you need to recuperate.

Make your personal day happen. Wishing for a day of fun and escape isn't enough. Planning your own dream day may be the incentive you need to make it come true.

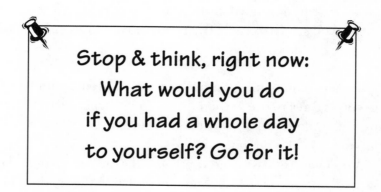

Stop & think, right now:
What would you do
if you had a whole day
to yourself? Go for it!

WILLIS FAMILY SNAPSHOT

Our typical, normal methods of managing naturally were funnier to those who never could imagine our particular brand of childhood, but to us, they simply gave structure and color and meaning to the phrase "one of the Willises."

I remember our weekly visits to the A&P. We had special relationships with vendors from early on. When I was young, I thought those relationships were based on the sheer volume of our consumption. Later I realized that Mom managed the volume by first managing the relationship—from the A&P to Ginsberg's Clothing store to Wechsler's. These stores gave Mom special treatment, because she treated those who worked there as special. At the A&P, Larry Mooney would pick out the best produce for us and then open a checkout line for the five or six carts we'd fill each week. Ginsberg's, Wechsler's and Milton Bodner's would open their doors for a few private hours before sale days so Mom could clothe the ten of us at special prices.

I guess the lesson I learned is that in the marketplace, it takes a village to raise a large family economically, and the family that gives to the village gets so much back in return.

—Fran

Large corporations often provide educational **seminars** for employees. The more important your position in the hierarchy of the company, the more likely such seminars, which allow a "meeting of the minds," will be one of your perks.

Continuing education is a must if employees are to remain productive, but parenting is a profession for which there is little preparation.

> ➤ You need to talk to other parents.
> ➤ You need seminars to exchange your best and worst moments of mothering.
> ➤ When you are at your wits' end, you need to know that others have been "there."

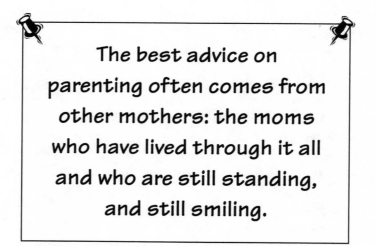

The best advice on parenting often comes from other mothers: the moms who have lived through it all and who are still standing, and still smiling.

Save the above statement . . . you may need it later. Give it to a friend. Use it the next time you hear an expert speak about parenting.

I don't believe that anyone can really teach parenting, not me, not even Dr. Spock. Even though I have ten children, what worked for me might not work for you. I say this precisely because what worked for one of my children wouldn't always work for the other nine. After more than forty years of parenting my own ten kids, plus twenty more years spent talking and listening to thousands of mothers in Mothers Matter sessions, I can't think of one absolute rule of parenting that will always work for everyone (except, of course, unconditional love).

Here's my thought: Not enough experts have personally survived cabin fever with two or three preschoolers, listened to siblings who battle constantly or actually done battle themselves with miserable adolescents. Many of the recognized experts have simply observed and analyzed mothers and then turned around and reported these findings back to the very parents who provided the data.

YEAH!

Okay, I'm sorry. Let me admit: It is not my intention to dismiss all experts so curtly. Of course, we need them. My dear departed father might just reach down and hit me on my head with his stethoscope. In medical dilemmas, experts are certainly critical. However, so many of the parenting dilemmas mothers face are not medical.

True Stories

How to Survive a Bonding Crisis—with a Little Help from Friends!

It was a Mothers Matter session in northern New Jersey, and the group of moms was very mixed in age and educational background. In fact, a grammar school principal with a six-week-old infant admitted joining the session simply to find someone competent to care for her baby boy. "I'm not the mother type," she said. She was well educated—some might call her an authority on kids, in fact—and wanted to hurry back to work as soon as possible. "I'm not planning to use up all my maternity leave," she explained to the other sixteen moms. "I'm not enjoying this new-baby stage at all."

A bit older than the others in the group, she had been sick for most of her unplanned pregnancy. Not willing to think that nausea simply goes with the territory, she blamed herself for the morning sickness, believing that her unhappiness about having the baby made everything even worse. "In the hospital, after delivery," she said, "when the nurses brought me my son, I didn't want to hold him. I was so tired. I only wanted to sleep. Now he's so fussy. It's my fault. It's because I never bonded with my baby right there in the delivery room."

She started to sob. The other mothers were quiet. I didn't say anything. No one spoke for several seconds. Then a young mother in a ponytail, wearing a comfortable sweatsuit, looked over at this experienced educator and said, "What did you say? Did you say that you didn't bond with your baby?"

> " I really learned it all from mothers. "
>
> —*Dr. Benjamin Spock*

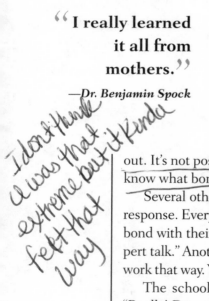

Before the principal could respond, this mom quickly blurted out with tremendous authority and confidence, "You don't *bond* with a first baby. You're exhausted. Wiped out. It's not possible to *bond* with your first baby. You don't even know what bonding is then."

Several other mothers laughed, and there was instant group response. Everyone agreed. First-time new mothers don't always bond with their newborns. Someone chimed in, "That's just expert talk." Another mom said, "Yeah, it's theory. It doesn't always work that way. You don't necessarily feel anything but tired."

The school principal dried her eyes. "Really?" she asked. "Really! Do you mean it? Are you serious?" If guilt were a visible weight, you probably could have seen it lifting from her shoulders. She had felt inadequate from the beginning, which had colored her every move as a mother.

As the evening ended, this educator approached me and admitted, "If I don't get anything else from this seminar, my coming tonight will have been worth it. I feel so much better." But her initiation into the secret society of motherhood didn't stop that evening. At the second session, she told the group that her baby had smiled at her. He was seven weeks old. "It was just the loveliest thing to happen," she said. The other mothers oohed and ahhed, remembering the awesome, heart-warming feeling of a baby's first smile. They understood and could relate to her joy.

At the last session, she announced that she would be taking her full maternity leave—perhaps even a little longer—so she could be with her son, the baby who had now become her joy. There was an immediate round of applause. The cheering was genuine.

> **"Anyone with preschool children should be compelled to leave the workplace by 5:30 P.M.—this means dads, too."**
>
> —*Kay*

Businesses often conduct **job reviews**. Are you sometimes so busy just functioning that you can't see what you are doing and why?

➤ If you slow down to ask yourself "Is there a better way?" you might come up with one. The process of reviewing—which good businesses consider critical—is one worth borrowing.

➤ Conduct your own review. Use this idea to examine your emotions as well as your obligations.

➤ Ask yourself: Why am I feeling this way? Or even: How am I feeling? What is it that I need to become a happier parent? What have I done right lately?

➤ No one else can possibly appreciate what you go through. Pat yourself on the back. Buy your own posies.

➤ Job reviews often signal the need for a shift of responsibilities. Is the work getting done on time? Or is there simply too much to do? If you were in an office or in the paid workforce, you would get help.

➤ Take stock of your stress. Are people expecting too much of you? Are you expecting too much of yourself?

> **" I used to schedule 'power lunches.' Now I take 'power naps.' "**
> —*Mother of two*

If the result of your review isn't **Yes, I am having fun being a parent!**, then look for ways to fix the problem.

An employee who works overtime or on weekends is often offered an option called **comp time**—free time to compensate for the loss of personal time.

➤ Put comp time into practice as a parent.

➤ Give yourself permission to nap the day after a long night of caring for a sick child.

➤ If you spend predawn hours mopping up a flooded basement, take the afternoon off.

A **quarterly report**, published four times each year, showcases the progress a company has made. Managers and workers can focus on the question "How are we doing?" Without a quarterly report, a business would be unable to see the big picture, the successes as well as the failures, but most important, where the company is heading in the future.

You'd be surprised by how refreshing this exercise can be for you as a mother. Your quarterly report doesn't have to be written anywhere but it should ask the question **"Am I having any fun yet?"**

Why is there a Secretaries' Week and only a Mothers' Day?

Once, when I posed the "fun" question in a session, a mom jumped right out of her seat and said, "I can't believe you asked that this morning. I was just waiting to tell you about my day yesterday. It was my daughter's third birthday. The theme of her party was 'Strawberry Shortcake.' Everything at the party was pink and red." She was excited. She was delightful. She had missed the point.

Meanwhile, she continued to describe each decoration in great detail. Near the end of her tale, she almost exploded. "The big surprise," she said in a voice growing louder and louder with glee, "was that I made a costume for our teenage neighbor, who suddenly appeared dressed as Strawberry Shortcake. She looked just like the *real* Strawberry!!"

> **Humor is a rich and versatile source of power— spiritual resource very like prayer.**
> —*Marilyn R. Chandler*

I have never seen the real Strawberry, of course, but I took her word for it. (*Is* there a real Strawberry Shortcake?) No one in the Mothers Matter session, especially me, wanted to diminish this happy mother's joy. Yet, when she quieted down, I did try to redirect her thinking. "That sounds just marvelous, yet I want to repeat the question: 'What is the most fun and exciting thing *you* have done in the last three months?' Think of something that doesn't include your kids." (She couldn't think of anything.)

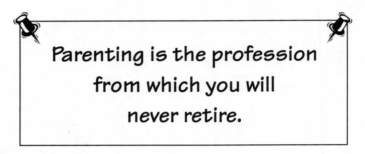

Parenting is the profession from which you will never retire.

Sometimes, as a mother, you are so busy planning and providing treats for your family —and enjoying doing just this—that you forget to consider yourself. You need to have fun.

Many businesspeople have an **expense account**. One of the hardest things for most mothers to do is to spend money on themselves. Admit it. While you may function as the chief purchasing agent for your family—bargain-hunting and buying everything from groceries, toilet paper, shoes and socks to underwear, and still managing to pay for dancing lessons, soccer camp and more, you have real trouble budgeting money for your own simple pleasures. I can't tell you how many years I wore "hand-me-ups" from my six daughters.

> " We do not stop playing because we grow old; we grow old because we stop playing. "
>
> —*Anonymous*

WILLIS FAMILY SNAPSHOT

The thing about growing up in a family of ten is that it seems normal when you're in the middle of it. It's only when other people make a fuss that you notice that you're different. So we endured people staring at our shopping carts at the A&P, the strangers asking us at playgrounds if we were a Brownie troop, the other kids counting us when we were in the car stopped at a red light, and the inevitable display of our Christmas picture at Levy Brothers, which used us as an ad for Santa photos.

> **" What do I want? Enough money for a haircut. "**
> —*Mother of two*

There is an upside to all of this. From a very young age, I was proud to be a Willis. I remember settling into dorm life at Georgetown and realizing that I had my own underwear. I was also angered by classmates who asked if I actually knew all the names of my sisters and brothers. (For the record, I can still recite names and birthdays, although I have to stop to figure out ages now.)

As the eldest (my father always used the word "eldest"), I got to observe the younger kids growing up. I could predict stages of development pretty well by the time Jerry and Danny cycled through. —*JoEllen*

Entrepreneurs are often advised to pay themselves first.

➤ Think about paying yourself a regular allowance.

➤ You are fiscally and physically indispensable.

➤ Consider how much it might cost to replace you.

➤ Create your own expense account—even if it only amounts to petty cash.

Think about it: When we don't succeed at parenting, other professions profit. Even big business has slowly begun to recognize the importance of good family life. I've conducted the Mothers Matter program on site for many of the country's largest and finest corporations, and an executive once admitted to me that when an employee's home life is in turmoil, his or her work is adversely affected. The end result can be higher absenteeism, a need for counseling and even an increase in medical costs.

> **" A mother is someone who can't remember the last good book she read but thinks it might have been *TV Guide*. "**
> —*Beth Mende Conny,*
> **A Mother Is**
> **Someone Who**

Repeat after me: "I make a difference . . . a big difference."

Kay Remembers . . .

The Business of Parenting

As the founder and director of Mothers Matter, I am actually a businessperson, an entrepreneur in fact. I have an exciting and satisfying career and have been the subject of many articles in national magazines and newspapers. I've traveled across the country several times and appeared on many television shows. I find it a hoot to sit in the back of a chauffeur-driven limousine on the way to a TV studio interview.

"You've come a long way, Momma!" Yet, for me, there's no business like parenting. Many times in my life, especially when I was eight or nine months pregnant and had a trail of little subordinates following behind me, I was offered sympathy. What I really wanted was admiration. I never felt the need for sympathy because I had so many children. Quite the contrary, I have always felt that my children were a blessing, and I took great pride in my work. I have had some extraordinarily grand moments and have very special memories because of my children. Now, after years of being the chief operating officer for our family, my workload is lighter than ever before. As chairwoman of my very own board of directors—my top ten advisors—I'm reaping dividends daily.

> " Pleasure is very seldom found where it is sought. Our brightest blazes are commonly kindled by unexpected sparks. "
>
> —*Samuel Johnson*

Think about it: Parenting is the only profession in which the raw material you are working with eventually becomes a human being. We are people-makers.

Make parenting a labor of love. The payback is phenomenal.

The very first time I saw Kay Willis in action, she was standing on a stage addressing more than a hundred people in a hotel ballroom. I was in the back row. I was working on a newsletter for mothers in the New York metropolitan area, and I needed a story with a message for moms. Kay certainly had one. Local news headlines had been proclaiming her to be a "professor of motherhood," "every mother's mother" and a "human development pro." Meanwhile, mothers in the audience were in awe of the persona of this woman on the platform.

Her words were wonderful, of course, but I sensed that it was her attitude toward being a mother that knocked them over emotionally. "Wow," we all wanted to say.

Ten years later, Kay and I are still exploring the attitude connection. We sit side by side at my computer looking at the simplicity of the idea. "This is too basic," I say. "Can the way a parent feels about herself really make this tremendous difference in her children's lives?"

"It is everything," Kay says, and then she adds, *almost* everything."

4. Happy Parents . . .
Know that Attitude Is Almost Everything

I often speak of the **AA of Parenting**. If you remember very little else from this book, I want this phrase to be locked in your memory. The first **A** is for **Attitude**. The second **A** is for **Atmosphere**.

> " I never screamed so much in my whole life as in the last five years. "
>
> —*Mother of two*

Almost everyone pays lip service to the importance of mothers—along with the proverbial apple pie and the American flag. I know you believe that mothers are important, but do you act on your beliefs? Do you command respect for your parenting?

I always think of a marathon runner when I'm searching for an example of someone with a great attitude.

➤ Look at the similarities between a runner and a mother.

➤ Both often begin working in the predawn hours, exerting their bodies to a degree that is beyond normal capacity.

➤ Both get sweaty and fatigued, and are sometimes even in pain.

➤ Yet both runner and mother persevere to finish what they set out to do.

> **" You never know what loneliness is until you have a child. "**
>
> **—New mother**

The big difference, as I see it, is that during a race, marathon runners draw crowds of supporters as they run along their twenty-six-mile route. Thousands of people watch their struggle, cheer them on, offer them water and, if need be, assist them across the finish line. Even the media cover the event so thousands more who admire the marathoners' stamina can witness their extraordinary physical feats.

Marathon runners believe in what they are doing. They inspire others to do the same.

True Stories

The Week Kay Dreamed of Being Queen for a Day

How well I remember the toughest week of my parenting life. I was pregnant with our seventh child. Five of our children had the measles. I was nauseous and throwing up every morning— often hoping I'd be sick before our children woke up. My husband was away on a business trip. My mom was in Florida. I was truly frightened, knowing that measles can be a deadly disease. Besides, both grandfathers had been on the phone warning me of possible side effects, including encephalitis. That's not all: *The clothes dryer was broken.*

Back then there was a television game show on every day called Queen for a Day. The woman with the saddest story won a prize. Each day, I would think, "If I could get on that show with my story, I could win the prize—a new dryer." But the show was in California. It wasn't my week. I was not in great shape. I was sick, tired, worried and also exerting extraordinary physical effort. Yet I was still in the race.

I think of that week each year when the New York Marathon is on television. Funny, but even on the worst day of that horrendous week, I never looked as poorly as those runners crossing the finish line. If I had, and happened to answer the front door looking as wiped-out and sweaty as those runners, I know I wouldn't have been greeted with a round of applause. Seriously, the person at the door might not have said a word about my sorry-looking state but, in fact, would have thought, "Look at her. She doesn't know when to stop."

I think I earned a gold medal for that week.

All mothers run a constant marathon.

➤ Do you give yourself the credit and respect you deserve?

➤ If not, can you expect others to do so?

➤ This is your race.

➤ Are you in shape?

➤ Are you psyched?

➤ Do you believe you can do it?

And by the way . . . If you are a stay-at-home mother, what happens to your attitude when you go to a party? Someone you've just met asks, "And what do you do?" Do you become a "used to be"? "I used to be a banker . . . a nurse . . . a secretary . . . a teacher."

Here's a fun story: One mom I met became so tired of defending her full-time role as a mother that she began to tell strangers, especially at parties, that she drove an eight-wheel rig. Word spread through the party, and many men came up to talk to her. "My husband was not too pleased, but I loved the attention," she admitted.

> " **I'd like to drive the good car.** "
>
> —*Mother of two*

➤ I used to be a "domestic engineer."

➤ When my husband was promoted, I became a "household executive."

➤ When I painted a room, I was a "set designer."

➤ In the laundry room, I was "wardrobe coordinator."

➤ And of course, I was continually seen by my family as "recreation director."

One day, my husband saw an ad in the classifieds from an eastern university:

Wanted: *Human Development Specialist. We are seeking someone with the ability to relate to the young, to in-*

*spire them and to motivate them to reach their highest
potential.*

This is a job description that fits parents perfectly. After all,
isn't this what we mothers do—relate to the young, inspire
them and motivate them to reach their highest potential? One
mother in a session became so excited about this idea that she
had her own business cards made up with "Human Development Specialist" under her name.

I am a

Human Development

Specialist . . .

and so are you!

Newspaper columnist Joan Beck once created her own
job description for mothers.

Wanted: *Athlete in top condition to safeguard tire-
less toddler. Needs quick reflexes, boundless energy,
infinite patience. ESP helpful. Knowledge of first
aid essential. Must be able to drive, cook, phone,
work despite constant distractions. Workday: fifteen hours. Will consider pediatric nurse with
Olympic background. Training in psychology desir-
able. Should be able to referee and must be unflap-
pable. Tolerance is chief requirement.*

❧ W ❧

WILLIS FAMILY SNAPSHOT

Just before my graduation from Tufts University in Massachusetts, I awaited the arrival of my entire family. As the family station wagon pulled up, I watched as my nine brothers and sisters emerged wearing identical T-shirts, emblazoned with "Kim Laude." (I was graduating cum laude.) My mother and father were also decked out in their own shirts as "Manager" and "Coach." I was already laughing as my mother handed me a shirt. "I'm Kim," it said. Traffic stood still along Professors' Row as people stopped to laugh along with us.

—Kim

 Other Mothers' Voices

From Career to Crib . . . and How to Answer Killer Questions

Three years ago, I was the youngest vice president of a big Madison Avenue public relations firm. I worked sixty to seventy hours a week. I loved it. And my zeal was rewarded generously: Fat paychecks. Trips all over the country. Chauffeured cars to and from work, when I deemed it necessary. Restaurant lunches, ordered-in dinners and lots of respect and camaraderie from people of whom I, in turn, thought highly. Day after day, I churned out press releases and pitch letters, attended meetings, solved one crisis after another—and I had energy left over.

Today, my hours are controlled by two precious and basically unprogrammable little humans. As a result, just getting to the grocery store can seem impossible, especially when I'm tired.

The killer question others pose is: "What do you do?" Another friend, who walked away from a flourishing career to be at home with her two children, confesses that she still finds herself saying, "Well, I'm a senior vice president of a bank, but um, right now, I'm on extended maternity leave."

It's been three years.

I describe my days of full-time motherhood to my husband by asking him to imagine running in water—with twenty-five-pound weights tied to his legs—during the monsoon winds. Yet I've never seriously considered returning to the office full-time since the birth of Kathryn nearly three years ago. For the most part, I delight in my commitment rather than doubting it. You don't get promotions when you're at home with children, but the affirmation you can get is profound.

> **" I've spent years simplifying my vocabulary so the kids around me could understand what I am saying. "**
>
> —*Mother worried about her ability to speak with adults in the workplace*

Billy was a month old and infinitely sweet-tempered. He'd lie in his Kangarockaroo forever, it seemed, while I cleaned or folded laundry or tended to Kathryn. I'd see him from across the room, teeny and still, staring blankly into the air. "He's fine; I have so much to do, just let him be," I'd whisper to myself.

But at some point, my conscience would finally win out. I'd put aside my task to kneel over this little person and talk. His reaction would knock me over—like a punch to the gut—for as soon as his wandering eyes found me, and drank me in, his tiny being came to life. The dullness vanished. A smile began in his eyes, and around his mouth, and grew and grew until it was delightedly huge. Arms and legs would pump. His eyes beamed an exuberant message: "Yes, I'm alive! I'm here! Thanks for asking!"

With Billy, really for the first time, it hit me: **I am everything to this person**. When I talk to him, he lives. When I walk away, he dies. My feelings weren't based on pride; it was awe. And I whispered a prayer: "My God, let me be worthy of this."

—*Anne Barrett Doyle*

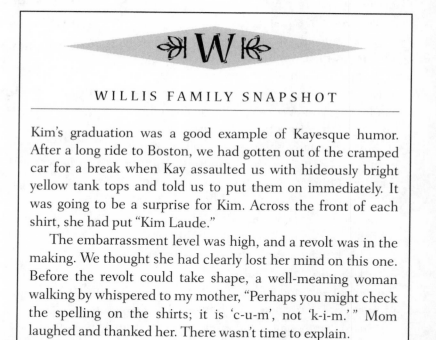

WILLIS FAMILY SNAPSHOT

Kim's graduation was a good example of Kayesque humor. After a long ride to Boston, we had gotten out of the cramped car for a break when Kay assaulted us with hideously bright yellow tank tops and told us to put them on immediately. It was going to be a surprise for Kim. Across the front of each shirt, she had put "Kim Laude."

The embarrassment level was high, and a revolt was in the making. We thought she had clearly lost her mind on this one. Before the revolt could take shape, a well-meaning woman walking by whispered to my mother, "Perhaps you might check the spelling on the shirts; it is 'c-u-m', not 'k-i-m.'" Mom laughed and thanked her. There wasn't time to explain.

Dad captured the event on film. A parade of hideous yellow in all shapes and sizes marching before the camera, all of us making that stupid, home-movie wave—you know the kind I'm talking about. I could not help thinking that someday I might look back on it and think it was funny. It only took about twenty years.

—*Jerry*

It doesn't matter whether you have three degrees in early childhood development or never finished school at all; your chances of success in parenting are directly related to your attitude about yourself.

Success means different things to different people. Some parents might want to point to standardized test scores, for instance. For me, success as a parent means raising a contented human being, someone who contributes to society and who still enjoys being in the same room with me.

" I'm busier than I've ever been, but I get less accomplished . . . no tangible evidence."

—Mother of four

All of my children have gone to college, and some have graduate degrees, but one of my greatest successes is the fact that they can still be in the same room with each other, as a family, and there are no fights breaking out. They enjoy each other's company as well as mine.

Kay Remembers . . .

Bag Lady Lessons

I was a full-time mother for more than twenty years. When Danny, my youngest, started school, we already had two in college, and there was a real need to supplement our already stretched income. I was looking for part-time work, preferably from my home. My sister-in-law, Elaine, a full-time earning-money mother for years, told me about a perfect opportunity. Someone was needed to oversee the luncheons being served in a private dining room for eight to fifteen people at the UN Plaza in New York City. No cooking, no cleaning, hours from 11:00 A.M. to 2:00 P.M. with excellent compensation. Most suburban mothers at that time wouldn't dream of commuting into the city for a part-time job, but it was more money for less time than I could find anywhere in New Jersey, and the hours were great. I got the job.

> " For me, the hardest adjustment of becoming a mother was getting used to being regarded as unimportant. "
>
> —Stay-at-home mother of three

After only a few days at work, I could see that huge amounts of money were being paid to local caterers for the luncheons being brought in. I also really had my eye on this sensational pie, piled high with creams and sauces. I was waiting for someone to refuse a piece so I could take some home as a special treat for my husband. When I mentioned this to my supervisor, she said she was tired of the bakery pies being served. In fact, she offered to order a pie just for me to take home. That didn't seem quite honest to me, so I bargained with her. I would bake any kind of cake she wanted in exchange for that expensive pie. The deal was made, and I don't know who was happier.

My homemade pound cake was so well received that I was soon making dessert every day. I must confess here that before this, with rare exceptions, I had always relied on cake mixes if I had any time at all to bake. The next thing I knew, I was offered the chance to prepare the entire lunch for the same atmospherically high prices being paid to the caterers. I jumped at the chance. I was still being paid my original fee for overseeing the dining-room preparations. The cooking brought in extra money.

Bonanza! At least, that's the way I saw it. Each night, after cooking and serving dinner for twelve, I would get the kitchen cleaned up and then begin preparing luncheons for eight to fifteen. I had never cooked gourmet food before. In fact, ketchup was the main accompaniment for my family meals. The world of herbs and spices soon opened up for me. I put wine and mushrooms in everything. I worked at this three or four days a week: In the morning, after the kids left for school, I would do the salads, icings and extra touches and then pack up everything in two see-through plastic shopping bags. Remember them? The kind with the daisies?

> " It is a parent's attitude finally, more than any physical act, that will change a child's behavior. You can do anything you want to, but in the final outcome, it's your emotional response that counts most. "
>
> —*Sanford Matthews, M.D., author and pediatrician*

Now, when I think about it, I can't believe I did this, but I did, taking the bus into New York with my bags in hand. I would walk more than twelve blocks across town.

One day, shopping bags on each arm, I found myself on Forty-second Street, just behind another "bag lady." The only difference was that my outfit was coordinated.

As luck would have it, our oldest was home from Georgetown University the following weekend, extolling the virtues of the new feminist movement. She was delighted with my new career as a caterer. "I'm so glad you've found yourself, Mom." I told her just where I had found myself: on Forty-second Street in New York City—a bag lady!

My real catering coup came when I was asked to tackle a Christmas dinner party for a hundred foreign exchange students.

Would I do it? Could I do it? My supervisor needed an answer as well as a menu right away. They were interested in serving something inexpensive, so I told them I'd serve Ziti Florentine (I had just learned that "florentine" meant spinach), tossed salad, French bread and a chocolate surprise. (The surprise was that even I didn't know exactly what I would make.)

> " **Motherhood is just an attitude thing—and a lot of unrealistic expectations.** "
>
> —*Anonymous*

When Christmas is coming and you have ten children to consider and you need money for gifts, you can get plenty of energy. I decided that I could cater this meal all by myself, and I did. It went beautifully; even the chocolate surprise was a hit.

What was so surprising? Well, I have very large cake tins—the kinds you might use for the bottom layers of a wedding cake. I used one chocolate cake mix for each layer. As soon as a layer cooled sufficiently, I put it in the freezer. Just before leaving for the city, I took out all the layers, so they defrosted only a little bit during the trip into New York. When I arrived, I iced the cold layers with Cool Whip and then covered the top with curls of chocolate shaved from a Hershey bar. Served cold, it was a huge success. Though I had repeated requests for the recipe, I never revealed my secret.

My reentry into the working world was a smashing success, but catering began to interfere with my real life: being a mother.

I had to find a better way.

"If I had the chance to do it all over again, I'd change very little about my life," Kay tells me one Wednesday morning. "I do think I'd try to be neater." She laughs. I tell her I don't believe her. She probably wouldn't change a thing.

"I'm from the school of orderly piles," she admits. "Some days, I would put the vacuum in the middle of the living room even though I had no intention of using it. If someone stopped by, I could say, 'Oh, I was just getting ready to vacuum.'

"My children were always more important than my chores," she says. "I do go for that 'lived-in' look. It's when my house starts to look like someone died in it that I have to get moving." I envy her relaxed approach to housekeeping.

Clutter bothers me. I need order so I can concentrate. I make beds. I clear kitchen counters. "Are you saying that kids thrive in messy homes?" I ask.

"No, kids thrive in cozy homes, where adults are listening and love is given unconditionally."

5. Happy Parents . . .

Create a Cozy Atmosphere

➤ Atmosphere in your home has absolutely nothing to do with interior decorating.

➤ Atmosphere has nothing to do with good housekeeping.

➤ Atmosphere is all about what it "feels" like in your home.

> **" Housework, when done correctly, can kill you. "**
>
> —*Susan Branch*

You create the atmosphere in which your children grow—physically and emotionally. It doesn't matter whether you work outside your home full-time, part-time or not at all. Mothers are usually the principal crafters of the home atmosphere. Fathers certainly contribute, but, more often than not, it is the mother who creates the emotional climate of a home.

Atmosphere and attitude are what I like to call the AAs of parenting. I stress them constantly because you need to store these AAs of parenting somewhere in your busy brain so you can retrieve them often. Lock these concepts into your memory: The atmosphere in your home is probably the most important single contribution to your child's ultimate happiness and/or success.

> " **Remember *Little Women*? What made Marmee a beautiful mother was not that she did it all (she had a housekeeper, and the girls had their chores) but that she imparted security, serenity, wisdom and love. Therein lies motherhood.** "
>
> —*Marcia Cantarella, president of Mom's Amazing Ltd., NYC*

The Dinner Dilemma: Do You Like Being in Your House at Suppertime? . . . And Other Questions to Ask Yourself

I ask a lot of questions in Mothers Matter sessions. I'm trying to encourage everyone to open up and share their best and worst feelings about their own parenting skills. When I ask, "What's it like in your house at dinnertime?" there are always chuckles and groans. "It's a madhouse" is an answer that comes up repeatedly. If you hate being in your home—especially at dinnertime—chances are your children hate being there too. **FIX IT.**

As a decorator in your home, you want to design beautiful spaces. As a nurturer, you are trying to grow beautiful children. A good climate is essential.

Take a minute. Think . . .

➤ What's the atmosphere like in your home?

➤ Do you like being there? (most of the time, anyway?)

➤ How does it feel to you?

➤ Does it feel cozy? ("Cozy" is a word that is nearly extinct but is so fitting in this instance, don't you think?)

➤ Is your home emotionally comfortable? When you enter, do you breathe a sigh of relief or desperation?

➤ How does it feel to your children?

➤ How do they enter? If their day hasn't gone well, is there someone there to welcome them, to comfort them if need be and to enjoy them—even via the telephone? Is there someone who will listen and really hear what they may not be putting into words?

> **" A smile is a light on your face to let someone know you are at home. "**
>
> **—Anonymous**

➤ Would your child in trouble be afraid to come home?

➤ Do you know how to discipline with love? Can your kids accept your anger or disappointment, yet still know deep down that you will never stop loving them? (I know, I know . . . sometimes it's really tough to like them, but your love won't be affected by momentary emotions.)

➤ Can all who enter your doors be renewed, refreshed and refueled?

That's climate control at its best!

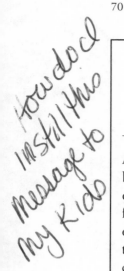

W

WILLIS FAMILY SNAPSHOT

As anyone might imagine, there were different prices to pay for being one of ten, as opposed to, say, one of two or three. One downside is simply a lack of clear individual identities apart from our relationships to each other. I imagine that from a parenting resource point of view, carving out ten separate identities would be a task more daunting and less important than creating a successful collective dynamic.

Overheard:

" **Oh God, are you home from school already?** "

—*Mother of three*

The important thing I've realized, however, is that my daily experience from very early on was that I was "special." That specialness was based on my Willis-hood. I spent my adolescence and most of my adult life fighting to illuminate why I'm special *apart* from my being a Willis, but I've learned over the years that one of the most valuable gifts my family gave me is the bone-deep certainty that I take into every single situation—that I am special, out of the ordinary and gifted. What a precious thing to know that simply by virtue of birth!

The flip side of that gift is the lesson that we are only as gifted as what we give. In fact, service is a key family value our parents taught us.

—*Fran*

Busy mothers with too much to do and too little time often long for the luxury of choice. Here's a thought for today: Exercise choice and skip the dishes.

You can use just the right words of praise, hang all their school papers on your refrigerator door, feed them all their vitamins, follow every expert's parenting pronouncements, but if the atmosphere in your home is cloudy or stormy, raising a happy child is not going to be any picnic.

> **" Children aren't fooled. They know we give time to the things we love. "**
>
> —*Author*
> *John Bradshaw*

Whether Conditions
(No, we haven't misspelled "weather")

Check your atmospheric conditions. A pleasant atmosphere depends on . . .

➤ **Whether—or not**—you are in good shape. Overtired? Overcommitted? Are you a center of calm or a storm filled with stress?

➤ **Whether—or not**—mealtimes are "hurry up and eat" occasions or relaxing family gatherings

➤ **Whether—or not**—you even have a dinner hour in your house

➤ **Whether—or not**—you sit down with the kids when Dad is not home for dinner

➤ **Whether—or not**—you sometimes treat your family just like company . . . with a tablecloth, good dishes, a special dessert and polite conversation (Really, does your family usually—or ever—engage in company-like conversation?)

➤ **Whether—or not**—your chores come before your children

➤ **Whether—or not**—you are up for anything that takes an extra few minutes

➤ **Whether—or not**—you have time to touch, stroke, admire, inspire or motivate instead of barely enough time to organize, feed, clothe, bathe, instruct and discipline

> " **I talk to them and tell them they are beautiful.** "
>
> *—Farmer Charles Rust, describing his gorgeous pumpkins*

➤ **Whether—or not**—stress is permeating the atmosphere

➤ **Whether—or not**—you are enjoying life or honestly still struggling just to get through, get finished and be done. Remember: Moms can't ever be done once and for all.

➤ **Whether**—your tone of voice is encouraging, commanding or condemning

➤ **Whether—or not**—you have a sense of humor. Silly time is time well spent. The family that laughs together comes together frequently and often—at least I have found that to be true in our family. For the last twenty years or so, every one of our adult kids has chosen to come home—from very near and very far—so we can celebrate Christmas together.

Ever hear yourself holler,
"Stay outside.
You can't come in.
I'm cleaning!"

WILLIS FAMILY SNAPSHOT

One of the funniest things my mother ever did was to dress Jerry as a lamp one Halloween. She used corrugated cardboard and taped a lamp shade to his head.

My mother was always able to defuse tension with her quick wit, which is an invaluable skill. She taught me the value of maintaining your humor even under the most stressful personal, professional and financial situations.

My first thoughts on growing up in a family of ten always seem to be about how that one block on Wood Street must have been the most fertile block in "middle-class suburban America." The Eberts, the Mannys, the Chaivellos were all large families. It wasn't unusual for thirty or more kids to unofficially close the street for massive games of kickball, football or whatever else we came up with. The large, stable, traditional family unit was the norm, not the exception.   *—Tim*

> **"Don't fall into the trap of thinking that you have to be good or even moderately successful at everything you do."**
>
> *—Michael LeBoeuf*

True Stories

A Perfectly Imperfect Home

When our children were little, I learned quickly that making a list of "to-dos" each morning was just an act of frustration, because by the end of the day, it had become a list of what I hadn't accomplished. The children were always more important than the chores. Of course, if I always followed that guideline, the chores could become overwhelming. Balance was the name of my game. I often referred to myself as Seesaw Marjorie Daw, the character in a familiar nursery rhyme. Just like Marjorie on the seesaw, I was either up . . . or down . . . but always trying to strike a balance. The kids had a way of demanding my attention, but the house continually shouted to me, especially when I had unexpected company.

> **" I need a doormat inside my house for the people leaving. "**
>
> *—Disorganized mother of three*

One day I found myself apologizing for the clutter in the living room, and my friend said, "Oh, I like seeing a house that looks lived in." My retort: "I don't mind the lived-in look, but when it looks as if I died, that bothers me."

I sometimes wish I had been a better housekeeper, but I never find myself wishing that I had enjoyed my children more. I truly can say, "I had a ball and I'd do it all over again in a minute."

➤ Orderly homes can be enjoyed.

➤ Trying to maintain an immaculate house, however, may create more stress than you realize.

➤ Stress pollutes the atmosphere.

I remember a mother in an upscale community in northern New Jersey who invited the Mothers Matter group to meet in her home for one of our sessions. This woman had insisted that I give her absolutes, specifics and "exactlies" during earlier sessions:

➤ "*Exactly* how much time should I play with my kids?

➤ When *exactly* should I do that?

➤ *Exactly* how am I going to find my two hours a week?"

Exactlies aren't my style. Exactly what worked for JoEllen would never be right for Patty, Kim, Maureen and certainly not for the boys. Every day, every child, every home, every mother is different. Attempting to answer someone with an exactly attitude is something I can never do.

I soon discovered the extent of this mother's exactness. Her home was absolutely perfect-looking. Her family lived in a model house. The only homey item in the living room was a candy dish. Absolute order and control reigned supreme over clutter. Even in the very large modern kitchen, the only thing on the counter was a crock of matching utensils. There were no magazines, no book bags, no children's toys and nothing warm or cozy about this home in the slightest. I was blown away.

> **"There is more to life than increasing its speed."**
>
> —*Gandhi*

When the going gets tough at home, and clutter concerns you:

➤ Put on popcorn

➤ Order pizza

➤ Meet a friend for breakfast

➤ Arrange a small vase of fresh flowers in your refrigerator

➤ Take a walk around the block

➤ If you can't leave 'em, join 'em in play

Question: Yikes! This is too hard. Too much of a burden. How can I be all this to everyone in my family?

Answer: You can't be—not all the time, but you stand a far better chance if you respond to your own needs first. Then you can better respond to your family's needs. With a little fun and relaxation in your life—regularly—your **attitude** about your own self-worth as a parent is bound to improve, and the **atmosphere** you create can become less stressful and more joy-filled.

Someone once said, "You can't go home again." I disagree. Not only can you go home again, but you don't ever really leave; you take the memory of your home wherever you go.

True Stories

A Laundry Basket for Me . . . and the Boys

For years all our vacations were spent at my parents' summer home. Packing for six or more children plus two adults required a studied plan. For luggage (this was before lawn-and-leaf bags became acceptable "travel" bags), I used a six-drawer cardboard chest, a laundry basket and one suitcase for Dad. Each of the girls was given a drawer to pack for herself. Everything they wanted to take along had to fit in one drawer. (When we arrived, they didn't need to unpack.) The boys and I used the laundry basket. Please remember, we needed space in the car for all the bodies as well as the luggage.

We traveled with five kids in the very back of the station wagon and three in the middle seat. I kept the old baby and the new baby up front with me.

> " **Whoever heard of Father Earth?** "
>
> —*Vance Bourjaily*

To this day, I marvel at my parents' generosity and patience. They shared that beautiful vacation home with their thirty-nine grandchildren—dozens at a time. The atmosphere was always welcoming, warm, relaxing. They had a neighbor at this lake house who was a self-proclaimed atheist. My Irish mother was a very devout Catholic and an exceedingly humorous woman. She often teased and joked with her atheist neighbor about their different points of view on religion.

> **"It isn't enough to be busy. Ants are busy. The question is: 'What are we busy about?'"**
>
> —*Henry David Thoreau*

One day, he came into her kitchen and said, "Nothing you've ever said has changed my mind about the existence of God, but that little granddaughter of yours came pretty close today." He had been watching all the little children racing around. Spotting our Fran, the only one in the crowd who had curly hair—and an extraordinary personality for a four-year-old—he called her over. "How come you are the only one with curly hair?"

Her response was immediate. "It was a gift from God."

Thinking he could trap her, he asked, "Oh really? What did the others get from God?"

Fran didn't hesitate for a moment, but plunged right ahead with her answer: "We don't know yet."

An orderly home can be a marvelous goal as long as the routine necessary to maintain that order doesn't exact an unhealthy price tag.

Kay Remembers . . .

Parachuting Toward Success

From my first experience in catering, I learned that homemade baked goods were always popular with people who didn't have the time, inclination or skill to bake, so I began renting tables at craft fairs every Saturday to sell my own baked goods. I would start baking tea breads on Wednesday nights, and all day long on Thursday and Friday my oven would be hot. Early Saturday morning, I would make as many yeast breads as possible before leaving for the fair. At that point, I'd have eighty to ninety loaves to sell and perhaps even a few cakes. By noon, I'd be sold out, with several hundred dollars in my pocket.

Baking was a lot of work—physically and emotionally. On Friday nights, I would line up all the wrapped and labeled breads and cakes on our dining room buffet, ready for Saturday's sale. Our tuna casserole never seemed to stretch far enough, and everyone would eye the goodies on the buffet. One night, after they had begged to eat one of my coconut pound cakes—a bestseller—I repeated my long-standing offer: "If it doesn't sell, you can all have a big piece tomorrow night." This wasn't what they wanted to hear, of course. The next thing I knew, they had collected enough money to pay for the cake.

Talk about guilt! I was always looking for a better way

> ❝ **I don't have time to feel. I'm too busy just doing.** ❞
>
> —*Virginia mother of three*

to make extra money without leaving home. My next career adventure was creating dried flower arrangements for local shops. In fact, my Christmas shopping bill worries were eliminated in 1975 when an agency ordered dozens of one-of-a-kind arrangements for all of their best clients.

Still, the money I earned never really compensated for the hours I spent in my basement storage room at night. There had to be a better way, and when I read *What Color Is Your Parachute?* I could see clearly something that had been right in front of me all the time. Described as a manual for job-hunters and career changers, this book's message was: Find something that you do well and enjoy doing. Well, I knew I couldn't keep on having babies—Lord knows, pregnancy and birth were things that I did well and enjoyed doing—but I wondered if I could help other mothers enjoy their parenting as much as I did.

This time, I conceived an idea, and we called it Mothers Matter.

> " **Make happy those who are near, and those who are far will come.** "
>
> —*Chinese proverb*

In the basement library of a grammar school, hesitant fathers choose seats around a conference table. It's 7:30 on a Monday night in the spring. Some have come begrudgingly, only to accompany their wives. Others are positively curious about Kay Willis. Three women arrive without men.

This is the fifth session of Mothers Matter and the first time dads have been invited. Coffee, tea and cakes are offered. Then, without much ado, Kay plunges into her subject: fatherhood.

"Do you know how important you are?" she asks these dads. Everyone agrees, of course. How could they disagree? Yet studies indicate that even average, loving dads spend less than eight minutes a day interacting with their children.

You can't make a lasting impression on a child if you aren't around to make it. Money isn't a true measure of your worth as a father.

To force these men to see the value of their presence, Kay asks them for happy memories of times spent with their own fathers. The room grows quiet. One guy starts to cry. His father has recently died, and the only thing he can recall is a long walk taken one night after dinner. "I'm sorry," he says.

6. Happy Parents . . .
Know that Fathers Are MVPs

➤ Dads are not substitute mothers.

➤ Dads are not babysitters.

➤ Dads are not pinch hitters.

➤ Dads are not relief pitchers.

➤ Moms are not the only real parents.

➤ In fact, dads are MVPs—Most Valuable Players.

Not every family consists of a mother and a father. We all know that—especially the millions of women who labor long and hard to raise their families single-handedly. I have also met women who describe themselves as single parents five days a week because their husbands work such extraordinarily long hours. But let's talk about the ideal for a minute.

Since most of us dream of the ideal life for our children, we must admit that the ideal is to have two parents happily sharing both the responsibilities and the joys of childraising.

Why Fathers Don't (Always) Act like MVPs

When my dad had his first child in the 1920s, not only was he not expected to have any hands-on experience with his baby, but any man of his generation who did would become the brunt of unlimited ribbing. By the time my husband became a father, there were still far too few men who were comfortable handling their own infants. Those who were, however, were no longer kidded as much and, in fact, were admired by some—mostly other mothers, I'll admit.

> " **One of the best things a man can do for his children is to love their mother.** "
>
> —*Father Theodore Hesburgh, Notre Dame University*

Let's face it: For generations, culturally speaking, childrearing was considered women's work. Moms, not dads, were considered the real parents. Men arrived home from work, put on their slippers and retreated into their newspapers. Women and children existed on another plane.

Today the scene has changed dramatically. I suspect there are many reasons for this shift, but at least two come to my mind: First, allowing fathers into hospital delivery rooms, so they can take part of their child's life from the very beginning, has had an effect. Most of their own dads were not present. Second, the return of so many mothers to full-time employment away from home has brought dads into closer touch with their kids out of sheer necessity.

Mothers may long for someone to share the work of parenting, but they haven't always been successful selling men on this notion of equal participation—not in 1920, and not in 1996. Here are just a few sales approaches that don't work.

Thrust a screaming child at a dad walking through the door and say:

- ➤ **"You try it and see how you like it."**
- ➤ **"I'm going out of my mind."**
- ➤ **"You've just got to share this burden."**
- ➤ **"He's your child, too, you know."**

How many women do you know who have to cry—literally break down and cry—for help? Crying is certainly and totally justifiable on many an occasion, but think about it: Why would anyone want to share work that was driving you crazy and to tears?

Too often, the adjectives and emotions you use to color the big picture of parenting are negative:

- ➤ Are your toddlers always terrible?
- ➤ Are your teens always horrible?
- ➤ Are you enjoying your role as a mother? If not, why should your husband enjoy it?

To make matters worse, fathers who do lend a hand often incur the disapproval of mothers:

> **"How sad that men would base an entire civilization on the principle of paternity . . . and then never really get to know their sons and daughters very well."**
>
> *—Phyllis Chesler*

➤ "No, not that way."

➤ "I don't dare leave you alone with the baby."

➤ "Those socks don't match her outfit."

➤ "You fed her *what*?"

Why (Some) Fathers Don't Think They Are MVPs

Every mother remembers her first day alone with a newborn. How frightened and inadequate we all felt! Eventually, you get the hang of caring for the newborn simply by doing it over and over again. Dads have the same awkward feelings and fears, but the more efficient a woman becomes as a mother, the more inadequate a father can be made to feel. Men who have never held an infant when they were growing up, and who were raised by absentee fathers, aren't going to know what to do. Instead of allowing men to get more practice tending the baby, some mothers relegate them to the role of assistant parent, and send them out on errands.

> **" The more things you care about, and the more intensely you care, the more alive you are. "**
>
> —*Arthur Gordon*

Why Fathers Are MVPs

I often kid about the fact that I had no sex education. It didn't take me long, however, to figure out that it took two people to create a child. I believe that nature intended—in ideal circumstances—that a man and a woman raise a child together not just because parenting is hard work, but because of the balance each sex brings to the effort.

➢ Money isn't the true measure of a father's worth. Yet the message to men that comes through the loudest and clearest—sometimes drowning out more important issues—is this responsibility to provide a good income.

➢ Your children will not judge you on your skills or by your mistakes. Kids will remember your motivation.

➢ Actions always speak louder than words.

"**As a rule, when happy lightning strikes, you aren't doing anything out of the ordinary.**"
—*Arthur Gordon*

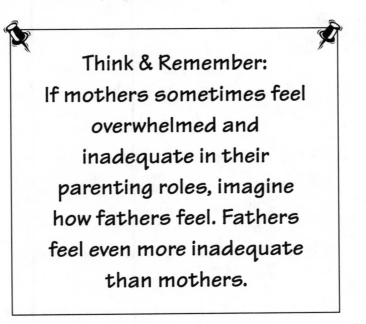

Think & Remember:
If mothers sometimes feel overwhelmed and inadequate in their parenting roles, imagine how fathers feel. Fathers feel even more inadequate than mothers.

**Copy this.
Give it to a dad:
Fathers are Human
Development Specialists.**

If you are in good shape, able to smile at your children and enjoy the fact that they are alive and in your life, you bring an unbeatable balance from the male perspective.

> ❝**No man is a failure who is enjoying life.**❞
> —**William Feather**

➤ You don't need to do everything exactly like their mother.

➤ You add another dimension entirely. Even unborn babies can recognize the difference between a mother's and a father's voice.

➤ You don't need to sound or act like anyone other than your own loving self.

➤ You should be different from a mother.

➤ You can reinforce a mother's message in every aspect of development.

➤ You complement and supplement.

➤ You aren't there to provide a carbon copy of the care a woman gives.

Above all, fathers are enrichers, not simply providers.

What Fathers Find Hardest

➤ "Not being able to read my wife's mind"

➤ "Second-guessing myself"

➤ "Switching gears when I get home from work"

➤ "Trying to figure out if I'm being too harsh or too soft"

➤ "Discipline: I have a hard time being tough."

➤ "The ten minutes before the school bus is due to arrive"

➤ "Patience"

➤ "Thinking of my kids as friends and my wife wanting me to think of myself as the disciplinarian"

➤ "Not being able to spend enough time with my kids." This is what I hear most often.

> **"There are many single parents doing a magnificent job raising their kids, but it is harder to do."**
>
> **—President Bill Clinton**

True Stories

Out of Work . . . But Not Ideas

When Bub and I were having our children, we felt safe in assuming that we would be able to send them all to college. Our lives were right on track. I loved what I was doing. His career in business was going well. Then, just as our first daughter began college, my husband, a senior executive in a large corporation, found himself on the unemployment line as a result of a managerial shake-up after a takeover. After months and months of job searching, all our resources were used up. We began to take on what felt like the weight of the national debt. Even after his return to work, with all the debts we had incurred, money worries were real, and college tuition money suddenly became a critical issue.

> " **When she calls me on the car phone and asks me how far I am from home, I know things are really bad.** "
>
> —*Father of four*

Yet all of our children went to college. Finding the way around financial obstacles wasn't impossible. Our ten were determined and creative. In fact, I honestly believe that it was because they had been given so much of Bub's time when they were growing up. A father's active presence in his children's life is as important as his earning power. Bub believed in our children, and because of this unwavering confidence in their abilities, they were empowered. They got wherever they wanted to go—on to some of the top colleges and universities in the country.

Lasting Impressions

In the Mothers Matter session, when I ask men to recall an occasion spent with their own fathers, the significance of fathers becomes clearer to everyone. Quiet times, words of praise, simple gestures leave the most lasting impressions:

➤ "I remember the way my dad used to praise me."

➤ "I used to help my father on Saturday mornings in the store."

➤ "My dad and I would walk to the corner paper store every evening together. Just the two of us."

➤ "My dad believed I could do anything."

➤ "I'll always remember the way he used to . . ."

➤ "I can't ever forget how he talked to me the night I . . ."

➤ "We would rake the leaves together every fall."

➤ "I remember how my dad would stand on his head and make us all laugh. We were so happy when he was happy and silly."

➤ "My father always carried me on his shoulders when we went down the street to the newspaper store."

➤ "He would let me sit in his lap and steer our car down the driveway. I felt so grown-up and proud."

➤ "Every summer night after dinner, we would take a walk together while my mom cleaned up the kitchen. I can still recall what it felt like to have my hand in his. The sound of early summer nights brings it all back to me, too."

➤ "He let me put his slippers on his feet. We would laugh together."

> **Giving bottles, baths, changing diapers and rocking infants are part of every new father's initiation into parenthood.**
>
> —*Sanford Matthews, M.D.*

A child who really gets to know his or her father, who connects with him and who feels loved by two parents, will have what it takes to get wherever he or she wants to be.

> # Helping children believe in themselves is a show-and-tell exercise. You've got to be there for them to believe in you.

True Stories

Daddy's Girls

There were certain daily routines that my husband couldn't bear to skip. He also wanted to spend time with his children, so he often included them in his favorite activities. When he walked in the door each night, he would reach for the mail first and then kiss us all hello. Then, before he could bathe the children in the evening, he had to read his paper. I can still remember seeing him on the sofa reading. Sometimes there would be one or two pairs of little shoes sticking out from under his newspaper. He would read aloud to the children about almost anything and everything in the news. He also loved sporting events on television.

> **"Two heads are better than one."**
>
> —*Anonymous*

Not only were our four boys encouraged to join their father's focus on news and sports, but our six girls all read the news and watched sports with their dad. As a result, our daughters know sports as well as most men—better than many, in fact. Kim and Maureen were the first female statisticians in Rutherford High School's history, because they knew various games so well. Jeane has built an entire career around her love of sports. As a sports producer for *Good Morning America*, Jeane covers all major sporting events from the Super Bowl, the World Series and the Kentucky Derby, to the Final Four NCAA Basketball Tournament games and the Olympics. Her dad was so proud of her.

A magazine written for busy, sophisticated career women in the eighties once surveyed the top hundred female money-makers at the time. Were there common denominators to explain their success? Could an assertive personality, a good education, heredity or family financial backing be the underlying reasons for these women's rise to the top of the executive earning heap?

Much to everyone's surprise, it was none of the obvious factors listed. More than 90 percent of those successful women described themselves as "Daddy's girls" because they had experienced wonderful relationships with their fathers.

If fathers knew that what they were doing was of tremendous value and everlasting in nature, they would focus more energy—or at least as much as they could squeeze from other life-sustaining tasks—on the effort.

Men don't often talk about what it means to be a father and rarely share the physical and emotional aspects of parenting. If they did, they might **Find More Father Time**.

One dad, who felt he had to go into his office every Saturday morning, started taking one child at a time with him each week. The special time spent traveling became treat enough to encourage good behavior at the office while he caught up. Lunch together was then the prize for both.

> " He spends all his time trying to give us the advantages of life. He doesn't realize that he's one of the biggest advantages. "
>
> —*Mother of two*

Another dad who rarely saw his children during the week came home for dinner with his "most important clients" at least one night each week. Very quickly, he started to discover his own importance, and to his family's delight, he was last noted trying for two dinners a week, according to his wife.

A shopkeeper whose busiest store hours were at dinnertime made it a rule to breakfast with the kids every day. In return, his older children started bringing dinner to the store.

Another father I met now comes home for dinner and then goes back to the office rather than arriving home after his children's bedtime. His wife likes this routine better, she told me, because she has some quiet time to herself. Their old routine called for two dinners each evening—one for the kids and another for the grown-ups—with all the late-night cleanup.

Question: How will your children recall time spent with their father?

Another good question: Do your kids enjoy being with their father?

Answer: The man who makes and finds time to spend with his children is giving them a message about their self-worth by realizing his own.

W

WILLIS FAMILY SNAPSHOT

Based on childhood memories, some of us are certain we were raised in different families.

Here is a favorite: Saturday mornings were Dad's time to take us with him as he ran errands. We'd go to Sam & Dan's for the newspapers and cigarettes, the barber shop, the dry cleaner's and sometimes to Andy Bobitz's house. Many of my memories are tactile, but none are more sentimental than the way Daddy would stand on the curb of Park Avenue and hold out his hands. Each of us would grab a single finger and, like an exclusive May Pole club, cross the street safely and securely.
                                                              —*Fran*

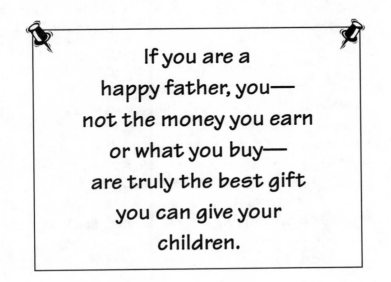

If you are a happy father, you— not the money you earn or what you buy— are truly the best gift you can give your children.

Kay Remembers . . .

How Mothers Matter Begin

A young mother and neighbor had three preschoolers when my youngest had already started school. She used to call me Mrs. United States Steel, because I had always appeared calm in crises. Diane Jones couldn't decide if I was totally crazy or a saint. (Let me tell you that having ten children negates any opportunity of becoming a saint . . . but crazy I ain't.) Diane was looking for support, and I used to tell her that having three preschoolers was more difficult than having ten in school. She wanted some of her friends to join us in our chats, so she helped to organize the first Mothers Matter session. There were seven moms. We sat in my living room one afternoon to exchange ideas and share concerns. After two hours of lively conversation, we decided to meet again. Humor and honesty flowed. We all complained openly and supported one another seriously.

We decided to meet several more times, and gradually new groups began. Word of my work spread. I called the local YWCA, and I was listed in the adult school's mailing. My daughter Patty helped me coin the name Mothers Matter. JoEllen proofread my brochure, sighing when she noticed that I'd typed "Kay Willis, mother of ten children."

"Think, Mom," she said. "Who wants to listen to anyone dumb enough to have ten kids?"

I considered my enjoyment of motherhood and my ten

children the best of credentials. It was 1975. We were in the middle of a decade during which so many new career options were opening up for women. It was also the age of specialization. There are special schools and curriculums for almost anything you want to study. In jest, I said to my six teenage daughters, "What's going to happen to you if you choose to become a mother? There is no place for you to go to prepare for motherhood—the most important, the most challenging and the most difficult career choice of your life. Although motherhood is no longer the only career choice you will make, it is still an incredibly important one. I don't see any 'How to Enjoy Parenting' courses in any college or university catalogs."

In 1978, I offered my first workshop for dads. Sixteen fathers showed up. Within minutes, I discovered that none of them had come willingly. They had been coerced or bribed by their wives. Yet the evening was so successful that I added a fathers' session to every Mothers Matter series. It's been very popular ever since.

Parents—both mothers and fathers—are much too important to be poorly prepared. Parenting, in fact, is not something you do with your left hand while your right hand does the important stuff. Parenting *is* the important stuff. Mothers matter . . . and dads do, too!

> " A surprising number of people seem to have come into being as a result of passion and laughter. "
> —*Robert Fulghum*

"Why does it take a tragedy to make us treasure our children?" Kay wonders. We've been talking of a young child in my town who was hit by a car and now lies in a coma—the kind of event that can paralyze other parents with fear. It also makes us focus suddenly on what a miracle this business of life is.

"Why do we wait until our children are sound asleep to stand by their beds in awe?" she asks. "Enjoy them when they are awake. Loving," she says, "means that we pay attention and listen well."

Kay Willis is at home on the telephone. Her children telephone her and one another from all over. They catch up, stay in touch, pass along news, call in search of support and share love.

Kay also talks to moms she has never met. They phone her from all across the country. She will always remember the woman who called in grief to describe the suicide death of her teenage son. "I didn't hear what he was saying to me," this mom lamented to Kay. "I just wasn't listening."

7. Happy Parents . . .

Listen, Listen, Listen

To be a good listener, all of you—your mind as well as your body—has to be there. Mothers suffer terribly from what I like to call "crowded brain syndrome." When your brain is crowded, there isn't room for anything else in there.

To listen, put aside all other thoughts. Concentrate on the speaker. Don't worry about chores. They won't go away. They'll always be waiting for you. Only then can you listen to what your kids are saying, understand what you are hearing, and acknowledge their feelings.

Have you ever tried to hold a conversation with someone who really wasn't interested in what you had to say? How did that make you feel? Have you ever found yourself just waiting for your turn to speak without really paying attention to what is

> **" Conversation at home has stiff competition."**
>
> —*Pepper Schwartz*

being said to you? I think we do this a lot to our children. They may be speaking, but we are waiting to tell them something. "Will you listen to me?" we ask.

> *"* **Raising kids is part joy and part guerilla warfare.** *"*
> —*Edward Asnew*

➤ We discipline them.

➤ We instruct them.

➤ We correct them and direct them— even criticize them.

➤ We do all or most of the talking so much of the time.

Yet listening may be the more important part of all conversation with kids. It is a time when we can learn about them— and even learn from them. I wish I had learned this lesson sooner with my kids. I was always trying to spare them negative experiences. I think if I had listened more, I would have discovered that they already knew much of what I was talking on and on about. I did hear "Really Mom, do you think I don't know that?" more than a couple of times. Not only would I have saved time, but I would have reduced the risk of turning them off.

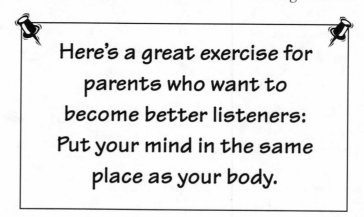

Here's a great exercise for parents who want to become better listeners: Put your mind in the same place as your body.

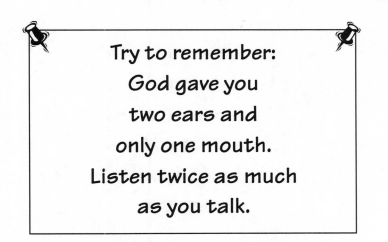

Try to remember:
God gave you
two ears and
only one mouth.
Listen twice as much
as you talk.

"Mommy (or Daddy), you're not listening!" Ever hear this before? Maybe it's because . . .

> You believe you can't spare the time to listen.

> You are trying to do two things at once.

> You aren't in good shape emotionally.

> You think you know exactly what your kids are saying, so you don't need to pay attention.

> You simply don't have time for the trivial. You have more important things to do.

> You don't realize that when you pay attention, you are saying, "I'm listening. I care about what is important to you." Your rapt attention is a gift of self-esteem for your child.

❝Parent-child communication is a process: trial, error, learn, observe, watch, make mistakes, regroup, back up.❞

—Ray Guarendi, Ph.D.

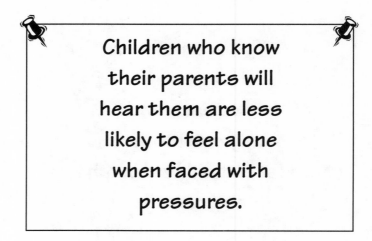

Children who know their parents will hear them are less likely to feel alone when faced with pressures.

➤ Research shows that fathers spend as little as eight minutes each weekday in conversation with kids, but moms don't do much better.

"Perhaps we never appreciate the here and now . . . until it is challenged."

—Anne Morrow Lindbergh

➤ If you are a full-time earning-money mom, experts estimate that your conversation time is less than eleven minutes a day.

➤ Stay-at-home moms spend only about thirty minutes a day talking with their kids.

How to Become a Better Communicator

Big business spends a lot of money training personnel in communication skills. No matter how extensive the course, one of the primary messages is always about eye contact. When you are talking to someone, your message will take on added meaning if you make eye contact. You will also be able to read whether this person is listening to you and comprehending your message.

Mothers fail miserably when it comes to eye contact with their families. Not only do we often talk to everyone with our backs turned (doing the dishes or emptying the dryer), but sometimes we speak from other rooms or holler from distant floors.

> ➤ If you had company seated at your dining table, would you stay in the kitchen preparing the food and shout to them, "Go ahead, I can hear you"?

> ➤ With a child, time for just the two of you is so important . . . especially if you have several children. Private conversations increase your chances of hearing wonderful revelations.

> ➤ "Know what, Mom?" is an invitation to which you should definitely RSVP.

> **" The word, even the most contradictory word, preserves contact—it is silence which isolates. "**
> —*Thomas Mann*

(When our Tim was about three years old, he used to stand up on the dining room chair next to me and grasp both my cheeks in his little hands. He had found a way to block out everyone else and get my attention. It worked.)

Create comfortable opportunities for communicating:

> ➤ Take one child at a time with you when you go out.

➤ Take the toddler with you to the basement and sit him or her on the dryer while you put another load in and fold the clean laundry.

➤ Perch on the edge of a child's bed in the dark at night; this is a wonderful setting for conversation. Most children will ramble on just to keep you there.

➤ Be a sitting target, and your kids will open up.

True Stories

The Pink Curler Connection

A mother in one of our groups shared her fondest memories of conversation with her mother. "I had three older brothers," she explained. "When I was still very young, my mom started inviting me into her bedroom for 'girl talk' whenever she set her hair. I would sit cross-legged on the bed and hold in my lap the shoebox full of those big plastic pink rollers women used for hair-setting. I would hand her the pink curlers one at a time while we chatted. Sometimes she would ask my opinion about something she was going to wear. As I got older, I knew I could talk to her about almost everything. She would always be listening closely to me when we had our 'girl talks.'

"I always hated to see that last curler go into her hair."

> **"What we are communicates far more eloquently than anything we say or do."**
>
> —*Stephen Covey*

To hear better than ever:

➤ Hang around your kids.

➤ Start early and don't stop. Communicating with kids is a little like staying in shape for a particular sport. You would never expect to be able to play tennis if you hadn't been practicing all along. Listening and conversing with your kids works the same way.

➤ Face your child when you speak and when you are listening. Square off shoulders with your child.

➤ Tone of voice is critical. "What" can easily turn into a four-letter word for a child. Angry? Wait before you open your mouth to speak. Being in good shape is critical. Think: Am I preoccupied, hungry, furious, frustrated or too tired to think straight?

> **"We work our way through it. If I listen to my teenage daughter and provide unconditional love, we always get wiser and more intimate."**
>
> **—Mother of a seventeen-year-old**

➤ Ask the right questions. Starting a conversation with the word "Why" will always put someone on the defensive, especially a child. Choose questions that will elicit more than one-word answers. Let your child in on something that happened to you.

➤ Share an experience. Ask for an opinion. Think back to what happened yesterday and follow up: "How did that go on the playground? What did the teacher say about your art project?"

WILLIS FAMILY SNAPSHOT

I remember driving in the Willis Mobile on the highway and having cars slow down to count how many kids were in the station wagon. I remember taking up the whole pew at Mass in St. Mary's Church. I remember the girls wearing matching outfits for every holiday. With hand-me-downs, I had the same dress years and years and years. I also remember walking down the halls of the high school and having a sister yell, "Hey, you're wearing my sweater!"

When we all became teenagers, I remember, it was cool for classmates to be invited to the Willis dinner table. Back in school, the reports were hysterical about the amount of food, the amount of noise, my father's deep voice and the topics of conversation, which included sex, religion and politics.

Perhaps this is where I first learned to be heard in a crowd. —*Maureen*

> **" I bet I spend two hours a day with my five-year-old, half an hour with my fifteen-year-old and about ten minutes with my sixteen-year-old. He's gone in a flash and then locked in his room. "**
>
> —*Worried mother of three*

Here's a tip: Preschool kids live in the now. "Tomorrow we will talk," "Later I can sit down," "This afternoon Mommy will have a minute for you" and "Next summer we'll be together" make no sense to a toddler. Some children don't begin to grasp such ideas until age four. For babies and little children, the concepts of past, present and future are disjointed. So watch what you say; your little ones may hear your words but not really understand your good intentions.

➤ Be a passive presence. Sit on the side of the sandbox. Watch a music video together. Read something aloud together.

➤ Establish a time in your busy life when your child knows you will be likely to hear. Working moms may want to consider an afterschool telephone appointment, for instance. One mother I know who had to spend long hours away from home didn't let her work keep her in the dark about her kids' activities. She would schedule her coffee break every afternoon at three o'clock and spend it with her kids . . . on the phone. They loved it. And so did she. It was the bright spot in the middle of her afternoon, and it helped her make it through to the end of a stressful working day.

> **" The majority of adolescents keep relying on their parents for advice and guidance even if they seem to resent it. It's crucial for parents to provide this. Withdrawal has terrible consequences. "**
>
> —*Dr. John Gottman*

➤ Be patient. Don't try to pull words out of your children's mouths. Don't finish their sentences.

➤ Don't always point out mispronunciations or grammar mistakes. Children under age six will often make mistakes as they meander through a thought or story while parents try to push a point. "Get to the end of the story," we want to say. Don't.

➤ Let your children own their own feelings. Don't try to talk them out of a feeling even if you disagree or fail to understand what the big deal is all about. Think back to the last time you were in tears about something and another adult said, "Oh I really wouldn't worry about it." You had a right to your own emotions, and so do your children. You can't listen clearly if you don't acknowledge how they feel.

➤ Put your paper down.

➤ Turn off the TV.

➤ Keep comments short. The fewer words you use, the more likely your child will feel comfortable having the conversational floor. (More than seven sentences in a row constitutes a lecture.)

➤ Don't start sentences with "When I was your age. . . ." This is not a great opening line.

> " **Manners are a sensitive awareness of the feelings of others. If you have that awareness, you have good manners, no matter what fork you use.** "
>
> —*Emily Post*

➤ Be a grown-up. Kids are notoriously good at dragging parents into verbal battles that can end up bringing out the child even in the most mature of adults. Even if you disagree with the logic, the facts or the reality of what your child is saying, don't try to win at all costs. Agree to disagree if need be.

➤ Get sensitive to prime times. You'll be able to hear what's on your child's mind if you set the stage and know what to listen for. Dinnertime, bedtime, sorting the socks, driving to the ball game . . . these are occasions when you can hear what is spoken as well as what is not spoken.

Kay Remembers . . .

The Willis Dinner Hour

Sometimes, when Bub was having a particularly stressful week, I would feed the children early and prepare a quiet dinner for just the two of us. He always objected to this. "I work hard so I can get home to be with them," he would complain to me. Our family dinner hours were always so important to him, as they were to all of us.

I used to call Bub "St. Grumpy" because no matter how much he wanted to be with his ten children, when things got a little crazy or the milk was inevitably spilled, he would roar like a lion. Yet, with rare exceptions, he was home for dinner with his family every evening. As I look back on those dinners together, I am sure they were a major contribution to our strong family connection. A lot was learned at the dinner table, a lot was shared and more often than not, there was a great deal of humor.

Our ten children sat in on important family matters, were encouraged to voice opinions and learned to listen to

> **"Never pass up a chance to keep your mouth shut."**
>
> —*God's Little Devotional Book*

one another. Because the children and I had been together for a good part of the day, Daddy always had the first turn to talk and to answer the question "How was your day?" Bub would really tell them about his day, in fact. The question wasn't taken lightly. Each of us, in turn, would tell something that had happened that day.

> ❝**I only came home for meals and snacks in the summer.**❞
>
> —*Mother recalling how important dinners were when she was growing up*

Sharing dinner at the table together was the one occasion every day when we were all on the same level. An infant seat was often the centerpiece, and the toddler was in a high chair. Everyone could make eye contact with everyone else.

For years we have been a source of wonder and amusement for high school friends, visiting college classmates and newfound adult friends when they join us for dinner at our extended table, which can seat eighteen, twenty or even more diners. There is a memory about our dining-room table for which my kids have never quite forgiven me. Our high school was sponsoring a local talent show as a fund-raiser. As committee members, Bub and I were having trouble convincing others to contribute their talents and perform. I decided that since we had always made so many people curious about what our dinner hour was like "with all those kids," it would be fun to do a mock scene of the Willis dinner hour. Onstage, two of the boys carried in oversized platters too big for any single person to carry. Exaggerated bowls and containers on a huge table set the scene further. We pumped up the noise level, too. It was hilarious. Naturally, our teenagers wanted nothing to do with the charade, but I insisted that our little play was being performed for charity. What's more, it would be fun. For years, they have recalled how mortified they were. At the time, I heard their objections, but I simply wasn't listening to their feelings.

Our dinner table has always been the core of our family unit, and I thank God for Bub's insistence that we meet there every day. If I were ever to be elected president of the United States, my first official act would be to make the family dinner hour mandatory for the whole country.

Do you recall that feeling on the very first night of your new baby's life at home in your care? I awoke to the sound of nothing, and my stomach lurched as I leaned over the baby's bassinet next to the bed. Still exhausted from labor, delivery and the shocking realization that I was responsible for another human being, I was checking for signs of life, of course. Was he still breathing? Oh God, remember when (pick one or add your own):

> Your toddler stepped off the curb into oncoming traffic and you were three steps too many behind
> Your five-year-old, feverish and limp, was admitted to the hospital for observation
> Your twelve-year-old dyed her hair purple
> Your sixteen-year-old didn't come home on time with the family car
> No one answered at home after school when you called from the office
> Fill in the blank with your own personal parental memory of fear _____

Fear is an emotion most normal parents know all too well. It's healthy. It can certainly save lives. Yet it can also color everything you do as a parent and ruin your chances for happiness.

8. Happy Parents . . .
Know When
to Say Yes

➤ "What a terrible time this is to be raising children."

➤ "Thank God, mine are grown."

➤ "I don't envy you one bit."

➤ "My lord, look what you've got to contend with—
drugs, sex, the AIDS crisis and that awful rap
music."

I know you have heard these statements . . . from almost
every corner of your life. **Don't you believe them!** There has
never been a better time to raise children. In spite of the stories, warnings, laments and statistics to the contrary, you have
so many advantages and so much knowledge at your fingertips

today. I have often said that if there had only been videos and microwaves, we might have had a big family.

There are always going to be evils in the world for parents to combat. Your grandparents worried about their children dying from polio, whooping cough and even measles.

> **Fear is the most paralyzing of all emotions. It can literally stiffen the muscles. . . . It can also stupefy the mind and will.**
>
> —*Arthur Gordon*

When my four boys were teenagers and New Jersey's legal drinking age was eighteen (it was later raised to twenty-one, thank goodness), I used to live in fear that one of them would use poor judgment and get hurt. Then I would consider my mother. During World War II, she had three sons fighting in the South Pacific when they were teenagers. That her children might be getting drunk was not her only problem. She was worried about their getting wounded or killed.

When your children are ill or in danger, fear is an appropriate reaction. Your fears can motivate you to do something about a problem, to head off a disaster or to take action. This is positive. Worrying is not always positive. In fact, parents today spend an awful lot of time worrying about whether they are doing the wrong thing or about what might happen to their kids. Worrying, in fact, seems to be the mark of a caring, responsible parent. It shouldn't. Saying "No, no, no" comes naturally to a worried, fearful parent. Knowing when to say "Yes"—and saying it as often as possible to your growing child—is a skill that can help them mature.

If there is one thing I learned from my experiences as a mother and from the happy parents I've met in the last thirty years, it is this:

Your children's
good judgment
does not come from
restraint but from
experience.

True Stories

Imaginary
Dangers

I was eleven or twelve when I came down with a mystery illness that lasted all summer. Late in August, a high, spiking fever even sent me to the hospital for five days. It seemed as if I would never regain my energy. Then, when I did finally recover, I was left with an irrational yet overwhelming fear that I would be kidnapped.

In those days, a common drama on radio mystery shows featured a criminal with a bullet wound forcing a doctor at gunpoint to remove the bullet. I had concluded that I would be kidnapped and held hostage until my father treated the criminal. For more than a month, I lived in terror. If my parents went out for an evening, they would be summoned home be-

" **Don't worry, be happy.** "

—*Meher Baba (popularized by singer/songwriter Bobby McFerrin)*

cause I was inconsolable. My mom was very patient with me, but finally, after weeks and weeks of dealing with my fear, she sat down with me to talk seriously.

"Kay, you have had a terrible summer and so have we. I wish I could guarantee you that you will never be kidnapped, but I can't. You know that the chances are slim to none that it will ever happen, but suppose you were kidnapped tomorrow. That would be horrible, but just think about how horrible this last summer has been. Wouldn't we be better off enjoying whatever time we do have instead of living in fear that something awful *might* happen? Let's thank God we are together and appreciate the gifts we do have. Don't waste the good times; worrying is a waste of time."

> **" Concern should drive us into action. "**
>
> —*Karen Horney*

I felt better and less fearful almost immediately. Not only did my mother's words lift me out of the depths of fear that summer, but they have stayed with me. I can't tell you how many times in my life as a mother those words have helped me through fearful times.

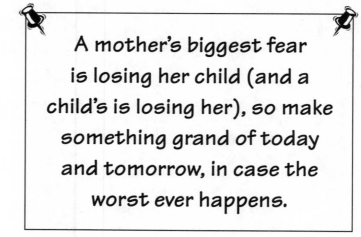

A mother's biggest fear is losing her child (and a child's is losing her), so make something grand of today and tomorrow, in case the worst ever happens.

Identify your fears . . .
and locate their source:

You yourself. Of course you have your own natural, normal worries to contend with. So did I. Yet, like my unfounded fears in that summer so long ago, many of your biggest nightmares could be based on imaginary scenarios. Yes, there are dangers. Yes, your fears could be real. But worrying will not get you anywhere. Worry is not a synonym for concern.

> **" Worry is like a rocking chair: It gives you something to do but it doesn't get you anywhere. "**
>
> *—Evan Esar*

Deal with the reality, not your imaginary disasters.

Experts. So much of parenting as taught by the experts today is based on fear. I call it the watch-out syndrome. Watch out, these experts say, if you don't . . .

➤ toilet train them right

➤ teach them right from wrong

➤ discipline them

➤ feed them nutritiously

➤ get the best education for them

. . . your kids could end up on a psychiatrist's couch, in the principal's office, with some dread disease or, heaven forbid, as failures.

The watch-out syndrome can ruin your fun as a parent because:

➤ Fear can color your every parenting move.

➤ Anxiety is not going to make you a better or more responsible parent.

➤ Worry can rob you of the joy of the moment.

Stress. Parenting is a dangerous job. I rank parents right up there alongside policemen, firemen and especially air traffic controllers. Parenting is stressful because:

➤ You have the responsibility for another person's life.

➤ You may be constantly on call.

➤ Danger lurks everywhere—even in the relative safety of your home, where curious children's antics can easily frighten the living daylights out of parents.

➤ Of siblings—no kidding! Your fears are probably real if you worry about siblings hurting each other and especially the new baby.

> " **Motherhood is the only occupation I know of where expanding knowledge causes self-confidence to shrink.** "
> —*Mary Kay Blakely*

Stress can magnify your fears and make it impossible for you to say yes to your child's normal, natural urges to explore. Rest is critical if you are in a stressful situation.

Are you getting enough sleep? Considering the stress of your job, just how alert can you be with the hours you keep?

Do you still have broken sleep because of a new baby, an "older" baby who hasn't learned to make it through the night, a sick child or teenagers out at night?

Is the word "nap" in your vocabulary? Maybe you are someone who can get by with little sleep. But is yours the kind of job that you want to just get by with? Isn't parenting more important?

The happiest parents I have encountered refuse to parent through fear. With each new age and stage of parenting, positive anticipation wins out over negative restraints. It's not that these men and women are fearless, or that their children are angels. "Cautiously permissive" is a better way to describe their approach. Their sense of knowing when to say yes comes from a variety of sources:

> **" I would like to put brakes on my teenager instead of braces. "**
>
> *—Mother of a thirteen-year-old*

➤ They understand their children intimately and can sense the demands of their ages, stages and social milieu.

➤ They know that they are the experts in what may be right or wrong for their children—not some other authority.

➤ They listen closely and can hear the signals kids send, indicating "Yes, I'm ready" or "No, I can't do this yet."

➤ They demonstrate a tolerance for generational differences in everything from haircuts to taste in music.

➤ What happy parents know better than anyone is that children need experience—a far greater teacher than they can ever be. As my mother used to say when I questioned something my children were about to undertake, "Say yes—if it won't make them sick or put them in danger. Trust them as much as possible, but, in the meantime, try to remove as many temptations and dangers as you can."

❧ W ❧

WILLIS FAMILY SNAPSHOT

One day, as Kay was straightening up the kitchen, a young neighbor burst in. Paul, who had recently moved into a house opposite the rear of our yard, was hysterical. "I'm sorry, Mrs. Willis. I didn't mean it, Mrs. Willis," he repeated over and over again. After figuring out that young Paul had hit her son Jerry in the head, she grabbed Paul's face between her hands and gently asked the sobbing boy, "Paul, where is Jerry?"

Paul pointed to the rear of the yard near the hedgerow that bordered the two yards. Dashing out of the house, Kay plunged through the bushes. Stopping to notice a baseball bat smudged in crimson red, she started to panic. Paul's older brother Otto pointed the way into the kitchen of their house. Somewhat taken aback, Kay felt uneasy. Mrs. J, Paul's mother, had Jerry bent over the sink and was flooding his copiously bleeding head with water from the faucet. Kay relaxed slightly when she saw that Mrs. J was attired in the crisp dress whites of a nurse. At that point, they bundled Jerry off for a trip to the family doctor and a few stitches in his head.

> **"The biggest problem with threats is that they tatter self-esteem and usually inspire fear or rebellion."**
>
> *—Adele Faber*

When the tale was recounted at the dinner table that evening, the story took a turn. Kay was horrified to hear from her youngest child that Mrs. J was not a nurse, but had recently purchased the local bakery.

—Dan

Listen to optimistic parents, and you'll hear:

➤ "Go ahead and try it, but be careful. I'm right here."

➤ "Okay, but I'm going to stand right here."

➤ "Yes I'm proud of you for trying."

➤ "Okay . . . What a big boy (or big girl) you are!"

➤ "Call me when you get there, and I'll know you are safe."

> **" It seems like all of us are so insecure and apologetic over what we are doing. "**
> —*Mother of three*

Do you understand your child's age and stage? Most kids can't be toilet trained until they are at least twenty months old, and most kids can't tie shoes until age four. Understand their maturity level, and it's easier to say yes!

When parents say yes . . .

➤ They stand by to catch kids but not to stop them.

➤ They encourage children to try.

➤ They allow children, who are ready, to test the waters of adventure.

➤ They don't magnify mistakes with "I told you so" remarks.

As a result, they help kids to believe in themselves.

Empty Words vs. Real Experience

How many of you have repeatedly told a toddler not to touch a hot stove? "Hot, hot," you say. "Don't touch." If a preschooler doesn't really understand what the word "hot" means, your warnings are meaningless. To confuse the issue even further, stoves are often cool, not "hot." The same toddler who touches a cool stove may doubt what you are trying to teach. I was always more inclined to let a toddler touch a warm stove—not hot enough to burn, but warm enough to demonstrate the notion of temperature—in order to base the lesson on real experience, not simply on my warnings.

> " **Motherhood is not all black or all white but it certainly isn't a rainbow either.** "
>
> —*Mother of four*

When you are trying to make a wise decision about any new experience for your child, you need to be aware of the situation (make it as safe as you can). You should know what your child comprehends, and you must understand your child's capabilities—then you can say yes with more confidence in the outcome.

Touching a warm stove, taking a spill down a little hill, balancing on (and perhaps even falling off) a garden wall, crossing a street alone, failing a test in school, suffering the consequences for having made a mistake (even a big one)—are the experi-

> **"We have nothing to fear but fear itself."**
> —*Franklin D. Roosevelt*

ences that teach judgment. Saying "No, no, no" is far easier and certainly less painful than saying "Okay, go ahead and try," but "Yes, yes, yes" will always offer more lasting lessons and will leave valuable impressions that can last forever.

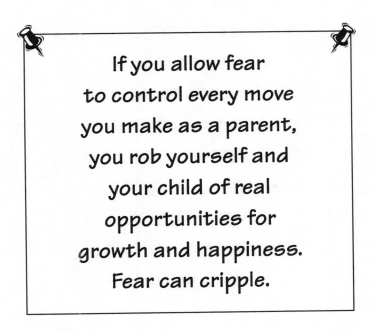

If you allow fear to control every move you make as a parent, you rob yourself and your child of real opportunities for growth and happiness. Fear can cripple.

One of the mothers in a Mothers Matter session was dismayed by her first-grader's lack of judgment. She sent him off to school one morning in a heavy rain but well protected, with a raincoat, hat, boots and carrying an umbrella. Unfortunately, when he arrived home after school and the sun was shining, he was wearing the same raingear—all of it. This mother was aghast and asked her son, "Why?"

"Because you told me to," he answered. He got an A-plus in obedience, but a Needs Improvement in judgment.

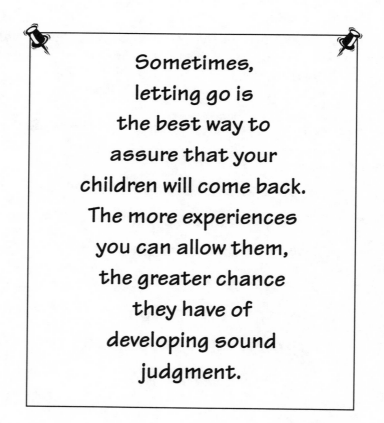

Sometimes, letting go is the best way to assure that your children will come back. The more experiences you can allow them, the greater chance they have of developing sound judgment.

When our ten children were growing up, especially during their teens, they lived up to my trust far more often than they did to commands, orders or rules. Children, in fact, will not do what you simply will not tolerate. If they are doing it repeatedly, it is because they can. Yet drawing lines over which kids are not allowed to cross only seems to invite them to dare you. A more effective approach—at least for me—was a healthy dose of trust, with a heap of praise and a dash of encouragement.

Keep in mind:

➤ Discipline and punishment are not the same thing.

➤ Discipline is a positive force. Disciplines are good for all of us. Discipline is a gift you give to your children.

➤ Punishment is a negative force.

➤ Well-behaved children give you better times.

> **" Is there a parent on earth who has not resorted to threats?"**
>
> —*Dorothy Foltz-Gray*

Can you see the Big Picture? Does your child see, too?

Can you imagine being asked to put together a complicated jigsaw puzzle without ever seeing the picture on the cover of the box? You might be able to figure it out eventually, but it would certainly take you a lot longer, and it would be a lot more difficult and a lot less fun. If you could see the big picture, you might enjoy the challenge and have a far better chance of success.

WILLIS FAMILY SNAPSHOT

The funniest thing I remember my mother doing is praying for the other football team's quarterback to get up after I had sacked him in a game. She didn't want me to feel bad for having hurt another player. We won. I felt great.

With ten kids, someone is bound to get left behind occasionally. We had spent a holiday at our cousins' house. It was time to go, and my family piled into the station wagon. The head count was taken—sort of—and off they went down the highway, sans me. I was left behind in the mix of eight other cousins. Someone finally realized that there was one too many kids still waiting to go home. A chase ensued. An exchange was made in the middle of a road . . . just like a Cold War spy transfer . . . except I was carrying a care package of petits-fours. For years to come, brothers and sisters tried to be left behind in hopes of getting another care package . . . just like mine.

If I had to choose one adjective to describe my mother it would be "motherful"!

—Ben

Children need to see the big picture of where you are heading them in life. Why you say yes and no becomes clearer to a child who "gets the picture." I used to try to help my children visualize their lives, especially their schoolwork, as a brick wall they were building. "Take the time to lay each brick the right way—one at a time. If you miss a brick," I'd explain, "there will be a gaping hole. If it goes in crooked, not only will it look awful, but it could weaken the wall. If your wall is wobbly, it won't stand up to the elements."

> # Children won't judge you on your mistakes—though they may remember and remind you of them; they will judge you on your motivation.

Kay Remembers...

Success on a Different Scale

In late 1977, my county government had unused funding earmarked for programs just like Mothers Matter. This money had to be awarded before the end of the year. I wanted this funding. Never having written a grant proposal, I simply described my program, applied and was quickly turned down. After more than a dozen phone calls to county offices trying to uncover the reasons for my failure, I finally spoke to a very rude man who told me that my proposal had been rejected because I had no "maintenance of effort."

"What is 'maintenance of effort'?" I asked.

He replied in the most condescending tone. "Honey, do you know what 'maintenance' means?"

" 'Maintenance' as in 'maintenance man'?" I asked.

"Yep," he answered.

Furious, I quickly retorted that even I knew that "effort" meant "to try."

"Now you've got it," he said.

"I do have 'maintenance of effort' in my Mothers Matter program. What can I do to correct this denial of my grant?"

"Reapply," he said.

> **" Sometimes an evil alien invades my body, pushing me to commit regrettable acts. "**
>
> *—Mother of two sons, ages nine and twelve*

So I did. On an exact copy of the proposal, I simply wrote at the bottom, "Maintenance of effort has been achieved and sustained." Within weeks, I was awarded a $51,000 grant for one year to open a center for mothers. One of the requirements was that I be monitored by an existing nonprofit organization, so I chose Fairleigh Dickinson University, my hometown neighbor in Rutherford.

Just one more step remained: I had to be classified by the county. What exactly qualified me to do this? Where did I fit in? The county official in charge of this classification process was a woman about my age who was simply incredulous that I intended to "teach" without a "teaching certificate."

"I'm sorry. There just isn't any way you qualify for this program. You don't have a degree."

What she didn't realize was that there just wasn't any way I was going to turn away from $51,000 and a chance to spread my message to other mothers. After forty-five minutes of debate, I convinced her that I was a "facilitator"—a category the county recognized and a word I learned for the first time.

Several weeks later, when the news media covered the opening of my brand-new mothers center, I was identified as a "Professor of Motherhood."

What a hoot! And what a title!

A Sunday evening in the fall and my phone rings. It's Kay calling from her dinner table in Rutherford. Her children—or a sizable number of them—are finishing up dessert and have decided to put together a list of their mother's worst mistakes as a parent. No kidding. They want me to know that, in spite of her position in the outside world as a parental role model bar none, she certainly made her share of mistakes when they were growing up. I hear silly laughter as the phone is passed around.

Stories emerge. A tale of inedible pink soup . . . a forbidden trip to Palisades Park with a seventh-grade class . . . Kay crying in front of the local school board as she pleads for an end to budget cuts. . . .

Number two daughter, Kim, tells me, "I was the only girl whose mother didn't understand."

"I never said I was perfect," Kay tells me. "In fact, being a perfect parent could be the worst thing you can do for your child."

9. Happy Parents . . .
Aren't Perfect

➤ Her children are always impeccably dressed, earn straight As in school and win all the sports awards. Yecch.

➤ She's president of the PTA, works full-time and never has a hair or hem out of place. Ooooh.

"Have patience with all things . . . but first with yourself."
—St. Frances DeSales

➤ You can walk into her home at any hour of the day or evening and not ever find dirty socks anywhere at all. Darn.

➤ She has never been called to the daycare center, the principal's office or the police station because of a child's behavior.

You ask yourself: If she can do it, why can't I?

Answer: You can't. She isn't. You shouldn't. You can drive yourself crazy with the illusion of the Perfect Mom. Yet that's just exactly what perfection is: an illusion! The perfection you think you see is only an illusion that someone else seems to have attained. Most of us know better than to compare our child to another child, but it is so hard to resist the temptation to compare ourselves to other parents.

You have no idea what any other mother may have going for her.

> ➤ She may have a mother living nearby who is always on hand when she needs help (or who drives her crazy).

> ➤ She may have a husband who says, "You look beat. Why don't you go take a nap, and I'll watch the kids."

> ➤ She might have a trust fund that allows her to buy those great outfits at the beginning of each season.

> ➤ I have even met mothers who like to clean.

> "The truth is . . . we mostly make do. That's how we run our lives most of the time. We might as well accept that. And feel good about it. And get good at it. It's a matter of attitude."
>
> —*Robert Fulghum*

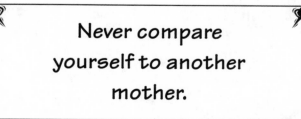

Never compare yourself to another mother.

We look at all these other more perfect mothers and wonder: How does she get everything done? A far better question is: Why does she need to get everything done?

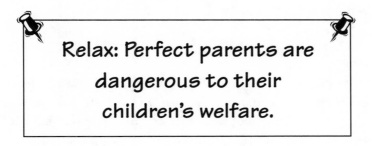

> ## Relax: Perfect parents are dangerous to their children's welfare.

I've met quite a few "perfect" parents, and they pay a high price for their perfectionism. Their families pay an even higher price. Not only is their striving for that impossible state of perfection exhausting, but it is also unrealistic. Perfect parents are never quite satisfied, and their dissatisfaction can even lead to depression—their own or their children's.

Think about it: If you believe that being perfect is the only acceptable standard, you are bound to become driven. Driven parents are critical of themselves and their children.

> **" It took me a long time to acknowledge that I wasn't happy . . . even though everything looked perfect from the outside. "**
>
> —*Mother of one*

You can catch "Yes, but" parents saying, doing and acting like this:

> ➤ A daughter arrives downstairs dressed for a party. Her mother says, "Oh honey, you look so pretty, but why didn't you wear the pink sweater?"

> ➤ A son hits a double to right field. "Wow, great going," the father says, "but if you choked up on the bat, you might have had a triple."

> ➤ A report card comes home with three As and two Bs. "What about this calculus?" the father asks. "What happened there?"

All children make mistakes, and some of those mistakes need to be corrected, of course. But living with constant criticism can kill self-esteem. **If you are never quite satisfied with your child's efforts**, he or she is less likely to put forth effort at all. It's easier not to try than to try and be criticized. Correcting a mistake is different from criticizing effort.

> " **Children are made of eyes and ears, and nothing, however minute, escapes their microscopic observation.** "
> —*Fanny Kemble*

> ➤ Give unqualified compliments. "You were great." Period.

> ➤ Always remember: Criticism deflates and diminishes self-esteem.

> ➤ To inspire and motivate your children to reach their highest potential, celebrate their efforts.

If you are never quite satisfied with your own efforts, consider the fact that giving your child an idyllic life isn't really a worthwhile gift. Children growing up in less-than-perfect worlds learn to cope better with the pressures of adult life. You simply do not need to protect your children from every crisis and every mistake. Sometimes, working through difficult situations or even dealing with an angry or frustrated parent prepares children for the real world. Seriously, do you want your child to grow up believing that nothing will ever go wrong and that you will always be there to nurture, assist and provide the comforts of life?

All families go through periods of dysfunction. Unemployment, trauma, illness and every new round of company layoffs and corporate shakeups all take a toll on even the most normal families. In fact, parents sometimes torture themselves in a quest to be consistent in dealing with their children. I firmly believe that being consistent is quite impossible. Don't try to be consistent. Be consistently normal. Your child's world is not going to fall apart because of your mistakes, your imperfections or your human frailties if you enjoy being a parent more often than not.

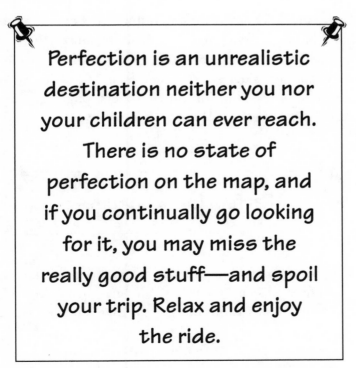

Perfection is an unrealistic destination neither you nor your children can ever reach. There is no state of perfection on the map, and if you continually go looking for it, you may miss the really good stuff—and spoil your trip. Relax and enjoy the ride.

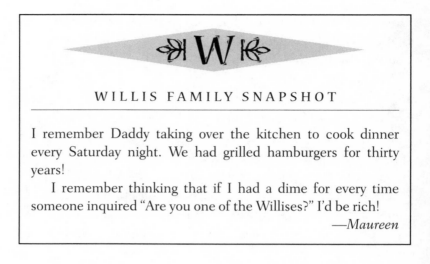

WILLIS FAMILY SNAPSHOT

I remember Daddy taking over the kitchen to cook dinner every Saturday night. We had grilled hamburgers for thirty years!

I remember thinking that if I had a dime for every time someone inquired "Are you one of the Willises?" I'd be rich!

—*Maureen*

Let's talk about stress for a minute. Stress and perfection go hand in hand. Trying to be perfect can cause great stress for yourself and everyone around you, especially your family. Some people consider stress a motivator and claim to work better under stress, but for most mothers, ongoing stress is negative and unhealthy. What's more, an overdose of stress can make you and your children sick.

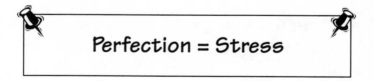

Perfection = Stress

The first step in eliminating stress, or at least reducing it, is to acknowledge its presence. You may have become so adept at dealing with your daily stress that you can't see it in your life.

Other Mothers' Voices

Coping Is Good;
Not Coping Is Better

That fall of my life had been exhilarating for me because of the special stresses of my job. The new year, I told myself, in the new year, everything would slow down to a more relaxed pace. Then I found out that I was being transferred. And then my doctor had other news: I was pregnant! Overplanning ahead, as working moms are apt to do, I figured that with a scheduled Cesarean, I could safely work to the last minute. I was young, healthy and had plenty of help at home with my five-year-old son. Then the housekeeper quit. I was still young and healthy, I told myself. I could cope; I would cope. I said this to myself over and over, like a mantra. A week into the new job, the doctor thought a miscarriage was likely. The circuits were overloading, and I was looking apprehensively into the mirror each morning for telltale signs of gray. The following Monday, my bus line went on strike: Thursday the new housekeeper quit; Friday, I decided that I, the great coper, couldn't cope.

> " **Burned-out kids often have burned-out parents.** "
>
> —*Anonymous*

That simple admission loosed a torrent of help. Within an hour, my mother was on my doorstep ready to take charge, to cope for me where I hadn't allowed her to before. What's more, my insistence on coping and on not identifying my stressful situation had kept other offers of help away. Suddenly, grateful friends—anxious to repay me for all the times I carted their kids to afternoon matinees and lessons—came to my rescue.

They had been there all the time, ready to offer a battery of help if I ever needed them. I needed it.

"Looking back, there were important lessons learned that year, lessons not generally afforded by perfectly smooth terrain. The valleys, the depressions, like shadows in a painting, highlighted the bright spots. Lesson learned: Coping is good; sometimes not coping is better. It forces us to reassess our strengths, reaffirm our relationships and take comfort in both.

—*Elizabeth Webbink*

Find Your Own Stress

➤ Do mornings find you juggling frantically between chores—waking sleepy children, making breakfasts, packing lunches, tying shoelaces, finishing homework, dressing for work?

➤ Does a residue of stress carry over from the night before? Did you have a late dinner? Is there milk in the refrigerator? Were you doing laundry until midnight?

> " **A bill marked paid can be a great stress-reliever.** "
>
> —*Kay*

➤ Teary children who don't want to go to nursery school, can't find the right outfit, don't know their algebra for the big test and won't eat dry cereal wreak emotional havoc on frantic mothers.

➤ Mothers, kids and car trips spell stress. I have stopped counting the number of times mothers in my sessions have admitted to automobile accidents. Have you ever turned to grab the bottle or toy that had fallen away from the baby in her seat . . . in the backseat of your car? Carrying carloads of screaming soccer players, listening to fighting siblings, feeling anxious about being late, spending more time looking in the rearview mirror than you do facing forward in a fast-moving car all put you and everyone else in your car in danger.

> **" The worst mistake you can make is to become overly concerned with making mistakes. "**
> —*Michael LeBoeuf*

➤ Okay, admit it: A "beat the clock" all-day, every-day schedule and an irrational need to try to meet all demands perfectly can make for stress!

Where does your stress come from?

➤ "From my neighbor. I live next door to the perfect mother."

➤ "From my husband . . . he wants things just so."

➤ "My job. The hours are so long."

➤ "Me. I was brought up a certain way, and I can't seem to stop."

➤ "From my kids."

➤ "When I read books about parenting."

Accepting your stress is not always the best attitude—if you can find a way to change or eliminate the source of your stress. I once told a group of mothers in a Mothers Matter session that I had given up making beds in my house.

Following an expert's
advice perfectly
doesn't make you perfect.
It just makes you
a follower.

One mom was aghast. "I couldn't live like that," she insisted. "I can't function if the beds aren't made." If making beds makes her feel good and she wants to spend her energy on this task, then that's fine. But for me, making eleven beds every day was causing me a great deal of stress and taking up far too much of my valuable time. I decided that it wasn't worth what I was missing. I made a choice. I eliminated so I could enjoy and have more fun.

More often than not,
mothers are their
own worst source
of stress.

I'll never forget the stress of grocery shopping on a budget. When my husband lost his job, trying to fit all our needs into a shopping cart limited to $100 was tough. I used to be afraid that people would think I was working in the store. I'd follow my usual pattern up and down the aisles, calculate what I had picked up and find myself going back around to return items I couldn't afford to the shelf. I still have dreams at night of not having enough food, and I always buy extra pasta and bread products just in case.

Grocery shopping isn't supposed to be a stressful activity by itself, but when you compound it with budget constraints or simply having two or three kids along for the trip, it can be emotionally and physically exhausting.

> " **My mother-in-law came to visit. I had cleaned for four days. She asked me if my husband and I argued about my housekeeping.** "
>
> —*Mother of three*

➤ Acknowledge this and other stresses.

➤ Pinpoint particular people, places or situations.

➤ Prepare yourself better.

➤ Plan more time.

➤ When you can't eliminate stress, anticipate and prepare for it. Eat before you shop. Rest before you drive carloads of kids. Leave early. Stop rushing.

True Stories

The Tyranny of a "Today" Pad

Have you ever seen those pads of paper on which each page is marked "Today," and there are about twenty blank lines on which to write your list of chores? I once splurged on one, thinking that it would help me organize my life better: The beds, the laundry, the vacuuming, window washing, grocery shopping, cooking were all on my list every day. (I never dusted. The dust never got a chance to settle in our house because of all the activity.)

I never used more than one sheet of paper in the "Today" pad. My list was the same every day, and I never reached the end. Talk about stress.

> **" Things which matter most must never be at the mercy of things which matter least. "**
>
> —*Johann Wolfgang von Goethe*

Later, I learned how to make the right kind of list. I write down only what I am sure I can get done on that day. The scope of my plans has been scaled down. Instead of writing "Clean the house," I'll mark "Clean one room." Instead of planning to "wash the windows," I anticipate "washing two windows." Meanwhile, every third or fourth line, I pencil in Interruption because I know I will be interrupted all day long.

At the end of a day, rather than being left with an unfinished list and the sense of a mountain of chores left undone, I can feel good about what I have accomplished. If I've been able to do more than one room or two windows, well, hooray. You have enough stress as a parent without adding to it with improbable, if not impossible, expectations.

Other Fathers' Voices

Not Just All in a Mother's Day

Bringing up children alone is one of the most stressful situations in the world, but the rest of us failed to notice. We just thought that was the way women are: emotionally scattered, edgy, out of touch. Well, they aren't. That's the way mothers are, whatever their sex.

After only the briefest exposure to the unrelenting fatigue, the enforced isolation, the emotional breaking and entering children specialize in, I found that I cared that I had to get up time and time again through the night to comfort a sick baby who had dragged me into terminal exhaustion the whole day before. I cared that just when I'd struggled to clean the kitchen, holding one kid in each hand, cooking with my forehead and holding the bill collector at bay with both feet—just then one child should soil the last clean overalls she had and the other should heave his spaghetti on the first load of laundry I'd managed to do in a week. I cared that I was sick of shouting baby talk and sleeping with two vomiting kids in a sea of mop-up towels. I cared that when I had a moment to myself, I needed it for crying.

> **" Know that you can't always solve your problems. You just have to know how to cope with them. "**
>
> **—*Anonymous***

> —*Robert Miner (a single dad who learned about "mother stress" the hard way)*

Kay Remembers . . .

Being an Expert on Bread— Sort Of

Because of my bread- and cake-baking reputation around town, I was offered the opportunity to teach breadmaking at the local adult school. I tried to turn it down. What did I know about breadmaking? Not much. Yet it was an emergency. The person scheduled to teach the course had gotten sick. The school had no one to replace her. Please, they begged. Won't you give it a try?

> " I couldn't have stayed sane without prayer and a phone. "
>
> —*Kay*

I am not qualified to teach breadmaking. I am a recipe follower with a good stove. The thought of attempting to teach basic techniques and skills overwhelmed me. Nevertheless, the school was desperate, and we needed the money I could make as a teacher. I said I would try.

Wonderful people take breadmaking courses. I felt right at home for the first two classes. On the third night, a man came up to me with a carefully wrapped slice of white bread. It had several good-size holes in it, and he wanted to know what caused the holes. I didn't have a clue.

Drawing upon basic parenting skills, I got myself out of what looked like a tight spot. "What do you think caused them?" I asked him.

He replied, "I think I used too much."

"That's a strong possibility," I agreed. "Why don't you experiment this week?" I suggested.

Before we met again for the next class, I found a book on the problems of breadmaking and planned to use it in my presentation. I also hoped to offer clues to the fellow's hole-y loaves of bread.

As soon as I arrived in class, he walked up to me, smiling broadly. "You were right," he said.

I told my husband the story later, and he asked, "He used too much what?"

When I explained to Bub that I never really knew too much what, he called me a fraud. The class later told me that they learned a lot. Believe me, I did too.

Nobody ever said I was perfect.

Though her ten children are happy adults ranging in age from thirty to forty-five, the question still pops up occasionally: "Do you have a favorite?"

"Yes," Kay is apt to answer. "But it changes frequently. Depending on what's happening, it can be the one who needs me the most or the one who simply asks me how I am."

We laugh about this. Kay is still the center of a whirlwind of activity in her home life.

Every mother and father—even those of us who had far fewer children than the Willises—know what it is to look at a child and think, Oh, she's my sweetheart. He's my little devil. She's so coordinated. He's so smart. She's always picking on her sister. He's trying to fight his way past his older brother.

These classifications and labels seem harmless. In fact, sometimes we assume that they are actually helpful . . . in determining our child's strengths and weaknesses—information that can make us better parents.

"Wrong!" Kay says.

10.

Happy Parents . . .

Know that Labels Can Stunt Growth

I had volunteered to become a religious education teacher for my parish church. It was mandatory that all new volunteers attend a series of five workshops, each taught by a different expert and offered once a week. The first and second sessions were really terrible. I would have quit then, but I was the designated driver in my carpool for the third session. I have always believed that being obligated to return for that third class was my good fortune.

> **Children are likely to live up to what you believe of them.**
>
> —*Lady Bird Johnson*

The teacher for this third class was a nun —a very irritable nun. Certainly not Miss Personality, she complained angrily that it would be impossible to provide us with adequate teaching skills in the two short hours she was allotted. I am sure she was right. After all, she had spent years learning how to teach. Nevertheless, she cared and had spent the previous evening racking her brain to come up with a lesson that could make a real difference in our teaching.

This was her lesson: "The most important rule I can share with you is: Don't ever classify your students. Don't label them. If you do, you will stunt their growth."

Okay, I remember thinking. I had heard this all before, yet I hadn't allowed the importance of the idea to sink in. She predicted: "By the end of your first class as a teacher, you will find yourself thinking, 'This is the troublemaker in the first row. This little girl is really the bright one. That one in the back row is a smartypants.' You may be fairly accurate at first, but children can fool you. When you label them, you put limitations on their development. Children have a way of living up to your expectations. You," she insisted, looking at each one of the volunteers, "can be a very powerful influence on your students. Be a positive one."

> " **Nature provides exceptions to every rule.** "
>
> —*Margaret Fuller*

I gave her lesson a great deal of thought . . . that night and for weeks and years afterward. I shall always remember it. I knew my own children. JoEllen was this; Kim was that. I simply had not realized the ramifications of labeling. I could see patterns already developing. Children grow and change if we let them. We must constantly remind ourselves to encourage them to keep growing and changing. Sometimes I still find myself, albeit unwillingly, falling into the labeling trap.

Labeling comes naturally to all of us. I remember how kids in grammar school used taunting and name calling: "Fatty, Shorty, Stinky, Stupid." In high school, we added the dimension of humor when we used a label unfairly. Family members sometimes make fun of one another using labels, but labeling is no laughing matter. It's a practice that can leave children scarred, inhibited and with a diminished sense of self-worth. Making a joke out of a derisive label will never make it right. And simply saying, "Aw, c'mon, I was only kidding" won't diminish the disastrous power of a negative label.

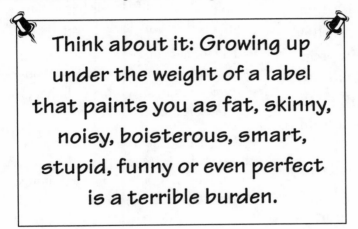

Think about it: Growing up under the weight of a label that paints you as fat, skinny, noisy, boisterous, smart, stupid, funny or even perfect is a terrible burden.

When you label your child, you send a powerful and sometimes permanent message about his or her capacity to achieve. Even though labels can be quite accurate at any given time, they won't be for long.

You can fuss over their vitamins, worry about their nutrition, read aloud every day and still stunt your children's growth . . . if you label!

> ➤ Labels limit.

> ➤ Labels imply that behavior is predictable. No child is absolutely predictable.

" I tell him again and again, 'Your brother's arm doesn't go that way.' "

—*Mother of two rival siblings*

➤ Labels are limitations that children will live up—or down—to.

➤ Children flourish when they are encouraged and inspired—not categorized or stereotyped.

> " **Does it seem impossible that the child will grow up? That the bashful smile will become a bold expression . . . that a briefcase will replace the blue security blanket?** "
>
> —*Anne Beattie*

➤ If children believe that anything is possible and that life holds happy surprises, they will act on these beliefs.

➤ The longer you perceive something to be true—no matter how erroneously—the less chance you have of changing your perception.

Even a good label can be a bad idea. High achievers, for instance, sometimes perceive even minor slip-ups as major failures. Applaud, cheer and expect the best from your children, but don't put them on pedestals that won't allow for easy falls. Making the honor roll, scoring the winning run, earning the lead in a school play are achievements worth working toward, or course. Learning what failure and loss are all about is also important. Wearing the label of someone who can do no wrong is a heavy burden for anyone to carry, even a bright, capable child.

Skirmishes in the Sibling Rivalry Wars

"How do I get them to stop fighting?" (This, by far, is one of the most frequently asked questions I've fielded in the last thirty years.)

Perhaps the worst perpetrators of labeling in your home are your very own battling children. Though you may worry about the physical wars siblings wage on each other, the wounds from verbal attacks can actually last longer and be far more harmful.

Bub and I never really stopped the fighting among our ten children completely. However, we did draw some very important lines of battle that helped to keep our home from becoming a war zone:

> **The walks and talks we have with our two-year-olds in red boots have a great deal to do with the values they will cherish as adults.**
> —*Edith F. Hunter*

> ➤ No punching.

> ➤ No hitting.

> ➤ No hair-pulling.

> ➤ Arguing was fine.

> ➤ Disagreeing was okay.

> ➤ Expressing anger was permissible as long as mean or belittling remarks designed to hurt weren't used.

My retort to any verbal abuse was to pull the offending child aside and say, "I won't allow anyone—not even you—to hurt someone I love." I considered our approach to anger a giant leap for me, because when I was growing up, my parents often said, "Stop your arguing. Nice young ladies don't get angry."

Surprise: Sibling Rivalry Is Not All Bad!

Several years ago, I was on a panel of experts discussing the ideal family size.

> ➤ The first speaker on the platform preached the benefits of having only one child.

> ➤ The second was going to discuss the advantages of having two children.

> ➤ My role onstage would be to explain why a couple should consider having three or more children.

It soon became obvious to me that no one was interested in my topic. This was an audience—primarily an academic group—that certainly could never imagine ten children being anyone's ideal family size. Humor would have to save me. In the meantime, the second speaker grabbed everyone's rapt attention when she launched into a description of the constant strain for parents in households with never-ending sibling rivalry. A psychologist, she was the mother of two adolescent daughters and knew what she was talking about personally as well as intellectually. (I hope you remember that I had six teenage daughters at one time. Yes, I said six.)

> **"There is no influence so powerful as that of the mother."**
> —*Sarah Josepha Hale*

Here's the good news I picked up that night and for which I will be forever thankful: **Sibling rivalry may be one of the best preparations for the real world any child can possibly experience**, this psychologist explained. Siblings aren't always fair, are very competitive, take no nonsense and can be mean and selfish.

Sounds like the real world to me, right? Children learn to negotiate, trade and drive hard bargains when they rival with siblings. Research shows that the more intense the rivalry, the higher the child's achievement level, so if you are the parent of siblings at war, hang in there.

I often repeat this piece of advice to Mothers Matter groups, but only once has one mother shouted in excitement, "Whoopee, I must be raising the next presidents of the United States!"

That psychologist's sibling message was so impressive that I suspect that at least a dozen or more parents conceived their second child that night.

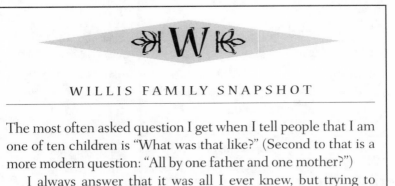

WILLIS FAMILY SNAPSHOT

The most often asked question I get when I tell people that I am one of ten children is "What was that like?" (Second to that is a more modern question: "All by one father and one mother?")

I always answer that it was all I ever knew, but trying to make people understand can be something simple. For instance, since I am the youngest girl, I wore a lot of hand-me-downs. When I went off to college and had a bit of spending money, I had almost every piece of clothing I bought monogrammed with my initials!

When I explain what it was like to have all ten of us travel in one Buick sport wagon, people practically go into shock. We didn't have today's strict child safety seat laws, so people find it hard to believe that sometimes when Dad drove, JoEllen and Mom would sit in front with Danny on Mom's lap; Kim, Patty, Maureen and Fran would be in their assigned seats in the middle; and in the "way back"

> " **Any mother could perform the jobs of several air traffic controllers with ease.** "
>
> —*Lisa Alther*

(which we always called the "deck"), Ben, Timmy, Jerry and I sat. It wasn't until I was much older that I really understood why my mother and father always began and ended our car trips with a prayer for a safe and happy trip.

—Jeane

Kay Remembers . . .

The Fighting on the Home Front

Our Ben and Tim are almost two years apart. I'd hate to count the number of times during their adolescence that I had to stand between them—literally—to stop their fights. It was not just a brief stage but a period of years that we suffered through these encounters. I used to pray that these two would grow up and move to separate areas of the country before they managed to scar each other permanently.

At any rate, things did get better. Perhaps it started the year they both played varsity football on the same high school team, or perhaps it wasn't until their college years, when they really did end up living in separate states.

The truly happy ending to this saga of intense sibling rivalry occurred on the night that Ben's wife, Madeleine, gave birth to Benedict Patrick Willis IV, my second grandson, in a New York City hospital. Five of our gang worked in the city at the time and arranged to meet at their favorite Irish pub. Ben's sisters were dying to know which godparents he and Madeleine had chosen for the new baby. Madeleine had already asked her sister, so the big question was: Which brother would be the godfather?

> **"You have a wonderful child. Then, when he's thirteen, gremlins carry him away and leave in his place a stranger who gives you not a moment's peace."**
> —*Jill Eikenberry*

Ben obviously wanted to speak to his choice in private, but the girls wouldn't drop their quest; their nudging and curiosity won out.

Later, in a teary midnight telephone conversation from the pub, I learned the details. "Mom," one of our daughters told me, "I wish you and Daddy had been here. Ben raised his glass and in an emotional voice began to speak of his great admiration and respect for Tim. He said that he wanted his own son to grow up just like Tim and to emulate his uncle in every way. Then he asked Tim to help him inspire Patrick and to become his godfather."

I was told that there wasn't a dry eye at the table. Even the Irish waitress came over to make sure everyone was okay.

It took Timothy a few minutes to collect himself, and when he did, he was very funny at first—typical of Tim. Quickly, however, he slipped into a speech in which he explained his surprise at Ben's admiration, because it was he who had always tried to emulate Ben's strength and integrity. The tears flowed again at the table in the pub that night, but even more so later on my pillow at home.

> **" Children grow through awkward emotional, physical and intellectual stages. By labeling them, we box them out of achieving their potential. "**
>
> —*John D'Auria, educator*

Kay Willis doesn't act like ordinary mothers I know. It's not just that she manages to stay calm amidst the natural, normal, every-day chaos of a wildly extended family. For a while, I couldn't put my finger on what exactly separated Kay from the rest of us. Then, one fall morning, we began talking about guilt.

Raise your hand if you feel guilty about something every day. Raise it if your children make you feel guilty. Admit that guilt is nearly a universal preoccupation for parents today.

Kay, meanwhile, doesn't ever act like a guilty person. This is amazing. This is the missing piece I've been quietly questioning.

"Spending time feeling guilty is not ever constructive," she insists. By refusing to let guilt control her actions, Kay isn't easily manipulated. She's absolutely straightforward. "Apologize and move on," she says to mothers.

Dwelling on past mistakes or on what a child, teacher, husband, wife, neighbor, friend, mother or father thinks you should have done or be doing is not helping anyone.

11. Happy Parents . . .
Know that Guilt Is a Waste of Time

➤ "You let your children do *what*?"

➤ "My children were never allowed to do that."

➤ "But Mom, everyone else is . . ."

➤ "Every other mother came but you."

➤ "Why can't you be more like . . ."

> " Give yourself no unnecessary pain."
>
> —*Percy Bysshe Shelley*

➤ "Well, my children are always in bed by 7:30."

➤ "The Smiths have two TVs."

➤ "We never go anywhere great on vacation."

➤ "I wish I had different parents."

➤ "I hate you."

_____ Fill in the blanks: When was the last time some-one made you feel guilty? What was said? Identify, identify . . . so you can acknowledge the emotion. This is your first step in freeing yourself of the burden of guilt.

If you are a mother, you probably feel guilty, and you aren't alone. My guess is that guilt is a universal emotion for parents. I'm lucky. My mother told me that guilt was a waste of time. "If you did something wrong, promise you won't do it again and get on with life. You aren't doing the children any favors by feel-ing guilty."

What is guilt, anyway? My *Webster's Dictionary* defines it this way:

> Guilt \ *'gilt* \ {*ME, delinquency, guilt, fr. OE* gylt *delinquency*}
> *1. The fact of having committed a breach of conduct esp. violating law and involving penalty— broadly: guilty conduct*
> *2: culpability 3: a feeling of culpability for offenses.*

> **" I remember leaving the hospital . . . thinking, 'Wait, are they going to let me just walk off with him? I don't know beans about babies. I don't have a license to do this. [We're] just amateurs.' "**
>
> —*Anne Tyler*

If Mr. Webster is right, guilt hardly seems to be an appropriate reaction for any mistakes or omissions on your part. If you did something wrong, apologize, correct the problem if you can and move on. Chances are you only think you were wrong. In any case, guilty or not, you aren't improving matters by feeling guilty. You are just making yourself and probably someone else feel bad. Is that what you really want to do? I don't think so.

Question: Where does your guilt come from?

Answer: I believe that all mothers receive a shot of guilt in the delivery room that can last a lifetime.

Question: Do you know why you always feel guilty?

> **"When you are a mother, you are never really alone in your thoughts. . . . A mother always has to think twice, once for herself and once for her child."**
>
> —*Sophia Loren*

Answer: You feel guilty because, in parenting, you are never quite sure that what you are doing is absolutely right.

Question: Who makes you feel guilty?

Answer: Just let someone comment, "You let your children do *that*?" and you can be instantly riddled with doubt about your judgment. What once seemed perfectly fine, no big deal, can suddenly become a major mistake. It's easy to make mothers feel guilty. Everyone does it. Grandparents, neighbors, teachers, husbands, children, experts all stand ready, willing and able to help you receive your healthy share of guilt.

No, I don't let guilt get to me. In fact, I made a deal with my children that has helped cut the guilt game down to manageable size. I tell them, "I will accept all the blame for the mistakes you make if I get to take all the credit for the good you accomplish."

I don't want to waste any more of your time talking about guilt!

> " **Women have a special corner of their hearts for sins they have never committed.** "
>
> —*Cornelia Otis Skinner*

**That's it.
End of discussion.**

WILLIS FAMILY SNAPSHOT

I remember the year my mom brought us costumes from F.A.O. Schwarz for Christmas. Patty was the fairy godmother. Maureen was a ballerina. Fran was a bride. I was a nurse. Ben was a policeman and Timmy was a fireman. They were so great. I can remember being dressed in red "feetie" pajamas but wearing my costume on top all Christmas morning. We had the most fun times around Christmas.

This is one of my fondest memories: Kay had a way of including us in her conspiracies of fun. For several years, the family was split between public and parochial schools so we chose December 8, a holy day, for our annual trip to New York to see the Christmas sights. We could all take the day as one of religious observance without getting an attendance penalty. Every other Catholic school child in the tristate area was in New York that day trying to see the same things. It wasn't much fun waiting on long, long lines and being pushed and shoved in the crowds. Soooo, the next year, Mom picked a day and called it Willis Family Day. Our notes to school the next day excused us because of a "family matter." All my friends thought it was totally cool that my mom would actually take us out of school to have a fun day.

—Jeane

Kay and I are talking about toilet paper.

"Every one of my children has gone to college, yet not one of them seems to know how to put a roll of toilet paper on the spindle," she says, with a bit of glee.

No, she isn't frustrated or resigned or angry. She laughs about this undeniable fact of her life. No one takes out the garbage in my household—no one but me, of course!

In fact, Kay and I confess that no one seems to understand what we mothers must go through. What responsibilities we must shoulder . . . carrying some of them so resentfully.

"If you don't meet your own expectations, you feel guilty," she explains. "But if others don't meet your expectations, you feel resentment."

"Which is more dangerous?" I ask.

"Oh, resentment," she explains. "Feeding your family a steady diet of resentment will poison everything you do."

"Poison?" I ask. "Isn't that a strong word?"

"Yes, but this is an important idea that calls for a strong image. 'Poison' is perfect."

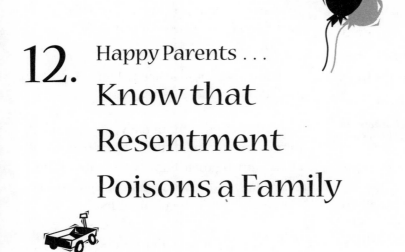

12.

Happy Parents . . .

Know that Resentment Poisons a Family

Resentment is a mother's greatest occupational hazard. You know what resentment is. It starts when you begin talking through clenched teeth. I call it the "Wouldn't you think somebody in this house . . ." syndrome.

Wouldn't you think . . .

> ➤ someone else could hang up a wet towel?

> ➤ he would call if he wasn't coming home for dinner?

"I laugh at what I used to think parenting was."

——*Mother of one*

➤ someone would realize the effort I put into keeping this house clean?

➤ he would acknowledge how wonderful I am to balance an impossible budget?

➤ they would appreciate all my efforts? some of my efforts? any of my efforts?

➤ someone would ask why I am lying flat on my face?

> **" It's not easy being a mother— if it were, fathers would do it. "**
>
> —*Dorothy, a character in*
> **The Golden Girls**

Overworked, emotionally overextended, unprepared mothers suspect that they are all alone carrying their burden. Oftentimes they are. No one else really does understand what you go through on a daily basis . . . unless you tell them, of course. How can they know?

Motherhood can be such a shock. Before our first child, JoEllen, was born, I remember dreaming of being a mother, but my fantasies revolved around layettes, bassinets, ribbons and blissfully happy scenes of home life. I was unprepared for labor, delivery and especially the days, weeks and months that followed. "How did my mother do this?" I would ask myself.

You just can't easily anticipate or understand what parenting is going to be like . . . until you are there. (I know I've said this before, but it deserves repeating.) When I had four preschoolers all day long—every single day—there were days I would find myself talking through clenched teeth. My mother would come to my rescue, insisting, "You need to go out and refuel, even if it is just for a walk to the five-and-dime store. You're filling up with resentment, and that's not fair to these little children."

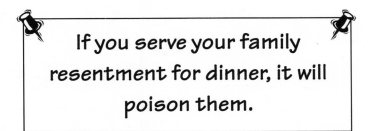

If you serve your family resentment for dinner, it will poison them.

Sometimes we mothers persevere, working diligently to reach the end of that long have-to list, for so long that we don't even know how uptight we are.

➤ Resentment is in the tone in your voice when you respond to the adorable toddler who will not let go of your leg and has been whining "Mommy, Mommy, Mommy" for at least ten minutes. Do you use four-letter words? Think not? WHAT!—in this instance—sounds just as shockingly strong as any other four-letter word shouted in anger. (If you are not resentful, you can stop a child's annoying behavior by crouching low and making eye contact the first time he or she whines, "Mommy." Answer softly, "What, dear?" and more often than not, the child will back off. Surprised by your immediate response, he or she may not even have formed a question at that point.)

"When people are behaving badly, when they are making a mess of things, often it's because they just don't have the strength to cope with their problems. They're not so much evil as enervated, not so much wicked as weary."

—*Arthur Gordon*

➤ Resentment is a spoiler. No matter how hard you are working, if you are filled with resentment, you negate your efforts. Your negative mood permeates the atmosphere in which you are supposed to be nurturing your family.

> Resentment can blind you. When you are overtired and suffering from fun deprivation—a dangerous disease that affects your whole family—you can't even appreciate a good thing when it happens. One young mother in a session told of how angry she was that her husband planned a whole vacation for the family in Hawaii without asking her. She didn't want to fly that far away with children and resented his gift. The other mothers—desperate for a vacation, even one with kids—had little sympathy for her.

> " **The quickest way for a parent to get a child's attention is to sit down and look comfortable.** "
> —*Lane Olinhouse*

> Resentment is a romance killer. Anger and love can't survive easily side by side.

> Resentment can make you physically sick. Think of your two hours away from home each week as preventive medicine. Truly, resentment is dangerous to your health.

> You can't raise happy children if you are resentful. They sense your resentment, not your love.

Is Resentment Growing in Your Home?

Is it time to ask for help? The most resentful mothers fall into two categories: silent sufferers or constant complainers. Neither path will get you where you want to be. Suffering in silence will only allow your resentment to grow wild, and complaining rarely gets positive results. You need to ask for help, directly and honestly.

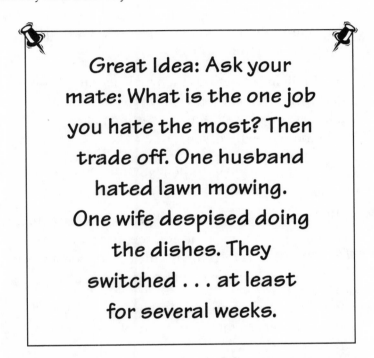

Great Idea: Ask your mate: What is the one job you hate the most? Then trade off. One husband hated lawn mowing. One wife despised doing the dishes. They switched . . . at least for several weeks.

Resentment can grow in your home because: You don't ask for much. You don't ask for enough.

When fathers face mothers in Mothers Matter session number five, I can't tell you how often these men say, "All you have to do is ask for help. What am I supposed to be, a mind reader?" (I know, some of you suspect that a father onstage is a father not to be trusted beyond his remarks. Yet, think about it, if you resent these dads' defense of their actions—or inactions—there is that ugly emotion once again. Resentment will poison your relationship with the man in your life as well as your relationship with your children.)

➤ Recognize your resentment—before you get to the "wouldn't you think" stage.

➤ Ask for help before you reach rock bottom. If you don't get it, you know it's really time for you to take care of yourself. You can't afford not to find a solution somewhere, some way.

> " **Know thyself.** "
>
> *—Inscription on the Temple of Apollo*

➤ You don't need permission to slow down.

➤ You don't need permission to protect some time and spend it on your own interests, on having fun, on romance or on a fun outing just for you.

➤ You don't need permission to take care of yourself first—so you can take better care of your family.

➤ No one wants a martyr for a mother.

Full-time earning-money moms and single mothers are even more in danger of getting caught in the resentment trap. There are only seven nights in a week, and you must be able to call one of them yours. Fatigue leads to resentment.

Are you saving babysitting for an emergency? Don't. Treat yourself to a sitter before you become the emergency and the cure becomes more costly than one night out.

WILLIS FAMILY SNAPSHOT

During the seventies, my mom and "the girls" all trooped off to see *A Star Is Born*. During the last reel, the projection went awry, and we couldn't see the lower portion of the screen during the emotional climax of the film. Kim, who was by then into assertiveness and other good feminist stuff (as we all were), marched off to the manager's office at the film's end. Mother, ever the protectress, charged from the rear. As Kim was making her case, Mom chimed in: "Yes, we couldn't even see Robert Redford in the death scene." Of course, it was Kris Kristofferson who died, but she made her point. The manager whipped out a ribbon of free passes for Clan Willis. —*JoEllen*

" He is in overdrive. I'm in overload. "
—*Mother of three*

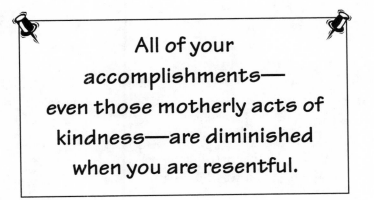

All of your accomplishments— even those motherly acts of kindness—are diminished when you are resentful.

Kay Remembers . . .

Paper Plates for Special Occasions

I love crafts. I also love making gifts for the people I love. For me, making something, even if it meant working late into the night in my basement corner, was not work, but the kind of activity that would renew me and make me feel good about myself. My mother used to become very angry with me if I took on any extra—and what she felt were unnecessary—responsibilities. Sometimes, in her zeal to save me from myself, she would suggest eliminating the very thing I needed to enjoy the holiday preparations. One of her favorite expressions was "Don't spread yourself too thin." Sometimes I would resent her trying to slow me down.

One year, as the holidays came closer and I was happily planning my craft projects, she begged me, "Please don't tackle anything extra this year. You're pregnant and you have more than enough to do. No homemade Christmas presents this year."

"Mom, why don't you ever tell me not to do the laundry?" I replied, a bit resentfully. "I'd rather give up laundry than the fun part of the holiday season."

"Well, find something you can give up," she insisted, "before you take on anything new."

Good idea! That was the first year I began using paper

plates every night for the weeks before Christmas. I still buy a large supply of paper plates whenever I'm planning a major celebration and use them before the party.

Take my advice: Give up something to make room for the good stuff.

Kay is telling me about one of her more memorable growth spurts. "It was my first venture back to college after more than twenty-five years as a full-time mom. One of the perks I received as a result of winning the grant for Mothers Matter in 1978 was free tuition at Fairleigh Dickinson University. I can still remember that first evening class," she says, laughing.

"What was so funny?" I ask.

"Everything and nothing," she explains. "I remember carrying a notebook and pencil to the class titled 'Women in Transition.' I was as nervous as any eighteen-year-old freshman might have been, but I soon learned that my sense of humor was as important as that sharpened pencil."

Kay's adventures in learning were full of surprises, but the most important knowledge she picked up that summer on campus was that her brain had not atrophied during all her years of full-time parenting. She could still earn As.

"My daughter Maureen is a teacher," she explains, "and she is always being reminded: 'Good teachers never stop learning.' I honestly believe that good parents never stop growing."

13. Happy Parents . . .
Never Stop Growing

I know so many mothers of my generation who kept postponing their own growth while they devoted all their time and energy to raising children.

> ➤ "My time will come."

> ➤ "When the kids are grown up and gone . . . then . . . I'll be able to focus on my needs."

> ➤ "Someday, I'm going to try . . ."

❝ It's my own fault that I'm not doing fine. ❞

—Mother of two

Their "time" still hasn't come. They are still waiting.

Timing is everything, not just in life but in parenting as well. Time, in fact, is on your side if you are a mother today. Did you know that the average woman is expected to live until age eighty-four? (No kidding. This isn't a number pulled at random because I'm an optimist but is, in fact, an actuarial prediction based on research by insurance companies.) If this ripe old age is true for you, you will spend a longer period of time *without* your children than you do *with* them.

Mommy, what do you want to be when you grow up?

➤ Are you still growing?

➤ Do you have any goals set just for yourself?

➤ What are you going to do with the rest of your life?

Great Idea: Instead of signing your kids up for class after class, why not use the money to hire a sitter, let them go to the park and you take a course in something fun.

In the fourth session of Mothers Matter, I ask moms to think about where they are going in life. I want them to think of themselves in both the near as well as the distant future.

Put yourself first for a minute right now. Think. Answer the same two questions I use in my program:

Question: What is your personal short-term goal? (What would you like to accomplish in the next three months?)

Question: What is your personal long-term goal? (Someday I would like to . . .)

At first, the answers for short-term goals center around completing projects—projects that are rarely personal.

> " **No thinking person can live well without reading and time for reflection.** "
> —*Alexandra Stoddard*

➤ To finish the kitchen

➤ To pack up the house so we can move

➤ To unpack from our last move

➤ To "get through" the upcoming holidays, vacations, school term break . . .

These women often find it difficult to focus on themselves. The litany of their lives is so often sung to the tune of "I just want to get done. I simply need to get finished. I have to get through." Is this you? Is this your constant prayer? A mantra you mumble working through your busy days?

Even when this session's discussion moves into long-term goals, mothers still can't easily accept the notion of something personal—rewards, adventures, ambitions, experiences, dreams—just for themselves.

Can you see yourself in any of these answers?

➤ To get organized, to feel in control again

➤ To learn to say no when I'm asked to volunteer

➤ To lose weight

➤ To start a disciplined exercise regime

➤ To go to a fat farm until I reach my goal

➤ To keep my sanity

> " **Being a mother, as far as I can tell, is a constantly evolving process of adapting to the needs of your child while also changing and growing as a person in your own right.** "
> —*Author Deborah Insel*

➤ To go to the beach and carry only my own towel

➤ To do Ireland on a bicycle

➤ To go horseback riding—outdoors. (This is an actual quote from one mother. I guess she was tired of rocking horses.)

➤ To have adult conversation—for more than a minute at a time

➤ To go to the supermarket alone. (This woman certainly needs to think bigger and to separate goals from chores.)

➤ To do something for myself during the day

➤ To go back to school

➤ To have an adult social life—now, I'm my daughter's social secretary for play dates!

➤ To have grown-up conversation with a man

➤ To slow down

➤ To take a nap

➤ To convince my husband to have a vasectomy

➤ To go out for dessert

➤ To be recognized as "a somebody"

➤ To find time to enjoy my children

➤ To learn how to make a reasonable to-do list

➤ To learn to list all the things I *did* do today

➤ To start a playgroup just for moms

➤ To learn ballroom dancing

➤ To start my own business

➤ To be a writer

➤ To get a life

➤ Not to have to cook dinner tonight

Have you ever noticed how free you feel on the days you don't have to cook dinner? Most of us don't take more than forty-five minutes to prepare a meal—if that—yet we feel so free on the days when dinner is not on our to-do list.

What are some of your goals?

➤ Write them down . . . now.

➤ Think big.

➤ Think often.

➤ Think fun!

> **"The better care I take of myself, the better wife and mother I am."**
>
> —*Mother of four*

Remember—if you don't have a goal, you certainly can't reach it.

Work—going back to full-time employment, switching careers, finding part-time jobs—are goals that come up often in

Mothers Matter discussions—and for good reasons. Statisticians often cite the fact that one out of every two women over age thirty will be responsible for her own income in ten years. Not only is the economy driving women into the workplace, but divorce, a husband's death, unemployment or disability are also changing the way women live. If circumstances forced you to change your lifestyle, would you be qualified for work you could enjoy?

> What is your earning potential?

> Would you prefer a different career path than the one you are (or were) on?

> Have you always planned to go back to school?

I've heard the most wonderful networking stories from women who have enrolled in courses for their personal growth. Read your community's adult education catalog. Send for a course catalog from the nearest college or university.

"The imagination is a muscle you can develop."

—Spanish director Luis Bunuel

There is no better time than the present to plan for your own long-term security.

> Be curious and courageous.

> Set a good example for your kids.

> Don't put your dreams aside . . . put them right out in front where you and everyone else can see them.

> More often than not, you will find wonderful people out there ready and willing to help somebody's mother get where she wants to be.

> **Get up and grow.**

WILLIS FAMILY SNAPSHOT

It amazes me how effective my parents were at conveying their value system to ten very different individuals. We all believe deeply in the importance of family, education, integrity and compassion for the less fortunate. Currently, some of these values have become politicized or rendered cliché, but my parents lived a life in which such virtues were manifest and re-inforced daily.

How were my parents able to give so much of their good-ness to so many of us with love? As I endeavor each day to do the same for my two boys, I realize how special, energetic and somewhat "crazy" they were to raise a family of ten. I am grate-ful that I was number eight (and number two son!).

—*Tim*

True Stories

A Woman in Transition

When Danny was about nine years old, I took a summer evening course at Fairleigh Dickinson University, which was right in my neighborhood. I was really not ever inclined to go back to college, even though I had been a reasonably good student. I didn't relish the thought of studying. How-ever, the university staff insisted that I take

> " Have they grown? Have you?"
>
> —*John Bradshaw*

advantage of the free tuition being offered to me as a result of my winning a grant and their sponsorship of Mothers Matter. I would be a good role model for the mothers in my program as well as for my staff.

Bub thought it was a great opportunity. I wasn't so sure. The most appealing course in the catalog was "Women in Transition," being offered in the graduate school curriculum. Because I had left college in my sophomore year, I didn't qualify. After a little perseverance on my part, the university allowed me to enroll because of my Mothers Matter program. I would earn three graduate credits and would not have to pay the $900 fee. I was blown away by the whole idea.

> " **Great living starts with a picture held in your imagination of what you would like to do or be.** "
>
> —*Harry Emerson Fosdick*

Off I went on the first night with a steno pad and pencil. The kids were laughing and teasing me. "Hey, Mom, you're trying too hard to look like a student."

The Rutherford campus of Fairleigh Dickinson featured classrooms in many of the large homes in the neighborhood. My class, in fact, was being held in one of these former homes, a block and a half from my house. I walked into a living room—not a classroom at all. There were only two or three chairs and about twenty pillows on the floor. A cocktail table was laden with all sorts of snacks and drinks—including wine! A very pleasant woman, who I later realized was the professor, nodded a greeting. This was not at all what I had expected. I had been worried about fitting into a desk.

More than twenty-five women and two men showed up for the class. The professor introduced herself and explained her relaxed approach to instruction. She asked for questions. I didn't even feel smart enough to know what to ask. Others spoke up, and questions about expectations and assignments were raised.

"Will there be a term paper required?" "Couldn't we skip the Friday evening class and stay an extra hour every other night?" The professor answered every query with the same question: "Why don't you vote on it?" I was more than a bit surprised and certainly didn't need a steno pad or a pencil.

Try to picture thirty adults lounging around on a living-room floor drinking wine and eating crackers and celery sticks while we voted on how class should be conducted. My anxiety about being a college dropout among graduate students rapidly vanished.

Our first in-class assignment was an exercise borrowed from a workshop our instructor had just completed herself and designed by the well-known psychologist Carl Jung. Directed to stretch out on the floor and close our eyes, we were told to imagine becoming a member of the opposite sex. (Was this the kind of *transition* the course title had indicated? I wondered.) Dimming the lights and speaking to the women students, the professor said, "You are growing hair on your face. Your arms are broadening, and your chest is flattening. Feel those muscles in your arms. Now, you are growing genitalia."

I struggled not to laugh out loud. Although it was dark in the room, I knew my fellow classmates would figure out that I was the "undergrad" who couldn't be serious. The next instructions I heard were "All right, sit up now and let's turn on the lights."

At that point, someone reported seeing a man's face in the window while the room was dark. I knew immediately it had been Bub. Worried about me, and not knowing our class had been extended an extra hour, he had walked over to escort me home. I could hardly concentrate on the three questions we were supposed to be answering: "Now that you are a man (or woman), describe how it feels to

> **"The most meaningful thing you can live for is to reach your full potential."**
>
> —*Deepak Chopra, M.D.*

1) walk down the street, 2) sit at your family's dinner table and 3) be in a bar."

When we finally rose from the floor at the end of class, I said to the woman next to me, "Is this pretty crazy, or is it just me?" She replied, "Imagine how I feel! I'm a nun."

I got an A. All my worrying had been a waste of time. When Bub asked me what I had to do to earn the A, I told him, "I grew the best genitalia in the class."

Kay Remembers . . .

Her Convention Just for Mothers

Most business organizations and professional societies sponsor conventions for their members. For years, one of my goals was to hold a convention for mothers. In 1984, I organized what the national press labeled as the very first convention for mothers. (In reality, a group called Mothers of Twins had been holding conventions annually for many years.) Nevertheless, I conceived my idea (conceiving has always been easy for me) in February, and with the help of my board of directors, my goal became a reality the first weekend in May.

> **Even if you are on the right track, you will get run over if you just sit there.**
> —*Will Rogers*

A novice at convention planning, I didn't realize that two months wasn't very much preparation time. (Most conventions are booked at least a year in advance.) Still, the Sheraton Hotel in Hasbrouck Heights, New Jersey, was really cooperative. Located only ten minutes from my house, they asked for a $400 deposit. I looked at my bank balance and said, "I can give you $84.00." They took it.

One of the most appealing aspects of a convention is that you leave your place of work and go somewhere with a relaxing, enjoyable atmosphere. You get together with your peers to share ideas and to discuss what is current, what works and what doesn't work.

I called and wrote to every local business and several national companies asking for support. Response was terrific. Every mom attending the convention received a free tote bag with more than thirty gift items donated. When the Associated Press picked up a report from our local papers about the convention, word traveled fast. I received calls and letters from all across the country, as mothers who couldn't come because of the distance wished me luck.

> **" Here I am in the trenches all day. "**
> —*Mother of four*

A $75 convention fee included admissions to all the activities and workshops as well as two meals. Hotel rooms were extra, but participants were encouraged to share accommodations to lower the cost. Certainly not an expensive convention, it was still beyond the reach of many moms. I had forgotten to figure in an important factor in my planning: Mothers don't have expense accounts.

With only two weeks left until the opening festivities, I came up with the idea of "motherships." Several of my children were attending college on scholarships, so why couldn't worthy mothers attend this convention on "motherships"? Twelve major companies came through. The first winner was a mother of thirteen who had never been away from home alone except for her hospital stays to deliver babies.

More than a hundred mothers from five states came together. I remember a grandmother, her daughter and granddaughter sharing one room. The convention received national media coverage, including the British Broadcasting Company (BBC). Featured on television were the Happy Hoofers, a tap-dancing troupe of mothers who performed in black mesh tights, spangled leotards and top hats.

We laughed and shared a lot at this giant sleepover. We had a blast.

Creative may be my middle name but I have never been a self-motivator—the next important step after having a creative thought. How many times have you said or heard, "I had that idea years ago. I should have done something about it then."

> " Living our own lives is not only a good example, it creates genuine community within a family, for community can exist only where people are free to be individuals. "
>
> —*Thomas Moore*, SoulMates

Most of my energy comes from need. You know the old saying "Necessity is the mother of invention." For me, necessity is the mother of my motivation, too.

Years ago, both my dried flower business and my catering career grew because I needed to supplement our income. Even after I started Mothers Matter, I would often feel pressured to give up and get a "real" job. It was at those moments, however, that I pushed myself to promote my program. Some giant steps were taken as a result of this pressure.

In fact, the periods of my greatest worries often produced periods of great personal growth.

Set goals. Don't ever stop growing. If I never had a goal, I'd be home alone now.

" **Success comes in cans; failure comes in can'ts.** "

—*God's Little Devotional Book*

"There is no such thing as quality time at 6:00 P.M.," Kay says. "I usually get a round of applause when I tell parents this."

Oh, no. Here is the old quality versus quantity time debate. Kay worries me. How can she say this?

"What about all the loving, working parents?" I ask. "Are you saying that their time with children in the evenings isn't valuable?"

"Not at all," she explains. "Quality time is an idea that has backfired. What comes to mind when I hear the word 'quality' is a tired mother trying to do crafts with cranky kids, or a woman pulling out flash cards while she stirs pasta, or families racing to the zoo. It all sounds so forced."

Giving your children the best of you doesn't call for elaborate family rituals at a time of day when most everyone is exhausted. It doesn't cost a cent or call for advance planning, either. This isn't the trip to the museum, the amusement park or the mall. Quality time isn't necessarily a parent reading aloud melodiously from the most recent children's bestseller. It's you—inviting your children to be part of your life . . . because you enjoy being with them so much.

14. Happy Parents . . .
Let Their Children
Get the Best of Them

Too few of us act on the knowledge that we are the most important gift our children will ever receive. If you are in good shape emotionally and physically, no one else will be any better at parenting your children than you. No one else has your motivation. No one else has your love.

> ➤ You may strive to give them advantages—a good neighborhood, the best education, music and dance lessons, sports—but these are all supplements, not substitutes for you.

> ➤ Raising children to be happy, contented human beings takes time—lots of your time.

> " **There is so much to teach and the time goes so fast.** "
>
> *—Erma Bombeck*

> ➤ Your **presence** is more important than any **presents** you will ever give to your children.

> ➤ Spending time with your kids is essential to their self-esteem.

Every child is a blessing. I sincerely believe this. Whether you choose to have children and carefully plan your pregnancies or have this blessing thrust upon you doesn't matter. What matters is that you realize parenting is the most important effort of your life. Treat it that way.

Choosing to make time for your children and to give them the best of you—right now, every day, time for fun, time to laugh, and nothing time, in fact—may seem difficult to a busy parent. Yet it's far less difficult than solving the problems caused by children's low self-esteem later in life.

" I spend more time in my kitchen than I do with my kids. "

—Mother of six

In recent years, self-esteem has been the buzzword in parenting and educational circles, and for very good reasons. The three most devastating problems of teenagers are suicide, pregnancy and alcohol or substance abuse. A child with a poor sense of self-worth is in danger of becoming a victim of any or all three.

Children who don't feel they are receiving enough attention will find a way to get it. They also learn very quickly that negative behavior often gets a quick parental response.

Did you know:

➤ Your child's positive self-image can be the direct result of your undivided and frequent attention.

➤ A child considered old enough to be left home alone may not be mature enough to appreciate or handle the solitude.

Ask yourself:

➤ How often are you home?

➤ How often are your children home with you?

➤ Do you spend regular time together as a family?

➤ Are you so busy that "leftover you" is on your children's mothering menu every day?

> " **Loving your children isn't enough if you don't enjoy their company.** "
>
> **—John Bradshaw**

Wait a minute. This isn't a problem confined to full-time earning-money moms. Mothers who consider themselves stay-at-home moms or who work part-time can also be caught in the time trap. Do you find yourself racing from day to day, expected to contribute time—and lots of it—to churches, schools, clubs, charities and health organizations? Eliminate. Eliminate. Eliminate. *Prioritize.*

We've become caught up with the notion that our children must be trained, disciplined and prepared for everything life might offer. We are also living in an age of specialization. When I was growing up, the word "specialist" simply meant an M.D. with special qualifications. Not anymore. Look around you. Today, specialists abound in every field—law, education, engineering, nursing, athletics. Even auto mechanics specialize these days. Busy, well-meaning, caring parents turn their children over to specialists all the time.

To improve schoolwork, you hire a tutor. To excel in sports, you rely on coaches. Camps of every design and description—soccer, ice hockey, basketball, computer, art, flute—put your kids in the hands of specialists.

Ask yourself:

> " **Shoot for the moon. Even if you miss it you will land among the stars.** "
>
> —*Les Brown,*
> **The Silver Lining**

➤ Do your children have a different specialist every day of their week—for nursery school, preschool and after-school music, karate, aerobic dancing and even play?

➤ Are your children overprogrammed? Are you?

No one can possibly prepare children for everything to come in their lives. Did your parents prepare you for computers? Mine didn't. The only way to prepare them for what life will thrust upon them is to give them the best of you.

It's only normal to want to enrich your children's lives and to give them the very best. If you are a full-time earning-money mom, there is a very real need to arrange constructive fun time for your kids when you can't be with them. Yet when children spend more time with specialists and instructors than they do with you, you aren't giving them the very best. Children need some "nothing" time—empty space in the day to daydream, to play, to create, to coast. They also need parents around.

Let's talk about quality time for a minute. In the 1970s, the theory behind quality time was a breath of fresh air that some moms desperately gulped. And why not! Women were heading into the workforce in droves, craving reassurance that it was okay to have a job and a family too. Of course it's okay. It's not only okay; life is often impossible to balance without two incomes. However, guilt was getting the better of everyone.

Someone came up with the idea of quality versus quantity time. If parents couldn't spend long hours with their children, then they were urged to put extra effort into the time they could be together. To make time "quality" as opposed to simply "quantity"—obviously, a less available commodity—mothers and fathers found themselves working hard to create idyllic occasions—even in the kitchen at 6:00 P.M. The now-famous "It's not the quantity of time you spend with your children, it's the quality that counts" quickly became gospel.

> **"Time, like a snowflake, disappears while we are trying to decide what to do with it."**
>
> —*St. Louis Bugle*

What's wrong with the idea of quality time?

- ➤ Quality time without quantity time will shortchange your children.

- ➤ The notion of quality time puts still another tremendous burden on you if you are a full-time earning-money mother.

- ➤ Quality time is an illusion at 6:00 P.M.—for *all* mothers (not just full-time earning-money moms) and fathers, and especially kids.

- ➤ If you are at home with your children, the notion of quality time is offensive. What would you call the time you spend with them?

➤ Quality time too often means that families are making appointments to be with one another.

➤ **Kids need a quantity of quality time!**

➤ Neat, perfectly controlled times together are not necessarily quality occasions.

> **" Day trips are such a disaster. Why do I want to do this over and over again?"**
> —*Mother of four*

➤ Even chaotic encounters can end up being fun.

Car trips, family vacations, trips to museums, parks, zoos, libraries or the movies can be great treats, but time spent together doesn't always have to be overloaded with meaningful experiences.

Honestly, quality time is:

➤ Anytime your kids have your undivided attention.

➤ Asking your adolescent for advice—about family plans, redecorating or what you should wear.

➤ Peeling an apple, offering a slice at a time while you chat with your child.

➤ Inviting your child to join you in raking leaves, shoveling snow or weeding the garden. Kids don't mind joining a parent in a chore as much as they mind working alone.

➤ Needing your children. Relying on them. More often than not, they will live up to your faith in them.

➤ Thinking like my grandmother, who used to say, "Treat your family like company and your company like family."

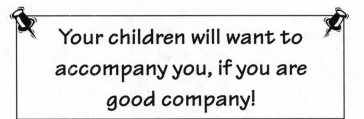

Your children will want to accompany you, if you are good company!

Children know what it means to be "company." "Company" is someone special. You treat company by using good dishes, baking a fancy dessert, conversing politely. Kids also know when you honestly need their help. Your challenge is to get your children to be both—good company and good helpers.

Other Fathers' Voices

My Dad, the Chore-Master

All my friends on the block thought my dad was a barrel of laughs. Our whole family had to do chores every Saturday morning, and no one was allowed to leave until the list was completed.

Dad would always promise to cook brunch for everyone who had helped out as soon as we were finished. Even our friends would join in, because my dad made it seem like such fun. He was a great pancake chef!

Dish Duty: A Meaningful Experience?

Strangers often ask me about how I managed to spend time with each of my ten children every day. Well, of course, I didn't always—at least not the kind of meaningful occasions that would land us in a quality time list of examples. In fact, dirty dishes were as likely to bring us together as excursions to New York City to see the Christmas decorations.

I remember when our dishwasher broke and we couldn't afford the estimate we were given to repair it. Instead of our usual routine of two children in the kitchen after dinner—one loading and the other taking care of counters and pots—we had to double up the work crew. Four kids pitched in every night, and I soon realized what a special time it became for them to be together.

> **" The more obnoxious your adolescents are, the more they need you."**
>
> —*Kay*

I would listen to them discussing school happenings or social events, chatting away. I didn't mind postponing the repair, in fact, because it was bringing our children together.

Just saying "I need you" to a teen can provide a real growing opportunity. I needed help doing those dishes. Too often we try to shield our children from the negatives in life, not realizing that the very issues we are so afraid of can turn out to be positive, though difficult, learning experiences for them. Looking back, I can see that during that prolonged unemployment period, Bub and I needed our children in so many ways, and they amazed us with their support and cooperation. They still do. Even today, my children have very diverse careers—from working in the ministry and gerontology to being a member of the New York Stock Exchange. We also have corporate officers, a teacher, a television producer, someone in sales, a very successful entrepreneur and an environmentalist. I am certain that the experience contributed to their successes today.

> **" Obedience training is for animals, not children."**
>
> —*Kay*

WILLIS FAMILY SNAPSHOT

Part of the wonder of Christmas in my life was the annual trip to New York City in December with my mom, to Radio City Music Hall. The pageant was a sight to behold. Long before the days of high-tech special effects, we were wowed by such amazing feats as the entire orchestra rising up from under the floor, actors and animals emerging from the walls and the amazing Wurlitzer playing Christmas standards.

On the streets outside, sometimes we discovered the true meaning of gridlock—human, that is. Once, we were trapped in an unmoving crowd and forced to listen to the holiday sounds of the Five Hundred Tubas. I remember a gentleman behind us yelling, "Pooosh!" We inched dangerously closer to plateglass windows. At this point, my oldest brother, Ben (then a tackle on the high school football team), sprang into action. In his most threatening voice, he said, "If you say 'Pooosh' one more time, I'll rip your head off." The man shrank back, and Mom patted Ben in a quiet thanks for keeping us safe.

As we emerged, Mom spotted two lost children. She told them to climb onto a station wagon parked in the middle of the crowd. She told them to flag down any passing cop they could see from up there.

> **"If I have done anything in life worth attention, I feel sure that I inherited the disposition from my mother."**
>
> **—Booker T. Washington**

—*Dan*

> # You don't need to give your children everything. You simply need to include them.

True Stories

A Jungle Gym in My Own Backyard

When my girls were young, we used to visit a neighbor who had a jungle gym in her yard. All the children would play together while the moms chatted and watched the backyard gymnastic routines. I couldn't wait until we had a yard big enough for our own jungle gym. I figured that I would be able to put the kids in the backyard to play and be able to get all my inside work done.

> "The thing always happens that you really believe in; and the belief in a thing makes it happen."
> —*Frank Lloyd Wright*

After our move to Rutherford, the new jungle gym went up in the yard. I was elated. My children loved it at first, but the minute I went back into the house to get something done, they would call me to come back out to watch them. They were happiest playing when I was in full view. It was me, not just the jungle gym, that created the playful ambiance. So I soon learned to combine work with play. Many a day, I took a laundry basket of clean clothes outside to fold or a pot of potatoes to peel.

Kay Remembers . . .

The Very Best Christmas Gifts

I have always loved Christmas in spite of the added effort it requires. What I haven't loved about myself is the way I've often succumbed to the last-minute use of charge cards, spending more than we could really afford on gifts I thought my children would flip over. The payments I made—sometimes until the following May or June—were rarely worth the attention these big-sacrifice items received. When I look back at photographs of Christmases past, the really special presents stand out:

The mini-stage we constructed in our basement. Using old plumbers' piping, we framed a plywood base big enough to hold three or four children. My mother's old draperies were perfect theater curtains. A spotlight and, later, a real microphone made this the gift that kept on giving back to us. The kids still talk about it.

An old trunk filled with dress-up clothes. This was in the spotlight the Christmas after the stage arrived from Santa Claus. It lasted until the old bridesmaid dresses (I cut them down to smaller sizes) were worn to shreds. Long skirts, tutus, a floor-length bridal veil, silk

> " Besides the noble art of getting things done, there is the noble art of leaving things undone. The wisdom of life consists in the elimination of the nonessentials. "
>
> —*Lin Yutang*

flowers for bouquets, wands, gloves and earrings made from jeweled buttons (which simply hung on loops of yarn over my daughters' ears) were all there for their fantasies. And the boys, who often converted the stage into a boat, donned the men's ties, suit vests, Superman capes, cowboy paraphernalia, hats and pirate scarves.

A working cash register. The incredibly popular accompanying attraction to this Christmas find was a stack of authentic brown bags from our local supermarket. Real grocery goods became part of the play, and our guests that holiday were furnished with real coins to give them purchasing power.

The appliance crate I took from a neighbor's curb. Wallpaper, fabric curtains, carpeting samples and eight-inch Ginny dolls found a home in the cardboard and wood crate that took my daughters by surprise. A few years later, I managed to locate a sturdy, very large dryer crate, and it became a perfect storage spot for new sleeping bags Santa brought my sons. The giant flashlight we gave them rather than a toy one has become a holiday memory, too.

> "**The Constitution only guarantees the American people the right to pursue happiness. You have to catch it yourself.**"
> —*Benjamin Franklin*

In the pressure of trying to be fair every Christmas to each one of my children, I also came up with this shopping rule: Get something huggable, something musical, something readable and at least one item that has never been advertised on television.

I keep a special "Christmas notebook" where I've listed

every gift I bought and for whom. Begun at a time in my life when Santa Claus needed help remembering which child received which gift from year to year, I find it a source of great joy today.

> " I never thought I should be rewarded for the greatest privilege of life. "
>
> —*Mary Roper Coker, Mother of the Year, 1958*

"What does romance have to do with parenting?" I ask Kay. "How can doing something romantic make you better able to care for kids?"

Kay answers, "The happiest parents I meet are the ones who have learned how to keep romance alive in their relationships."

These men and women are still talking and still enjoying each other's company. They understand that, for them, falling out of love isn't as much of a problem as making time for each other.

Putting romance back helps to recharge both mothers and fathers who need to see beyond the everyday mess and stress. Something can get lost in a marriage if couples are rarely allowed to escape from the kids, the kitchen sink, the unpaid bills, the never-ending load of laundry.

"Romance feeds the heart," Kay says. "Romance turns a casserole into a banquet."

Romance is essential!

15. Happy Parents . . .
Romance

When I was an adolescent, I overheard a joke that I just didn't get. Everyone else laughed. Later that evening at our family's dinner table, I decided to try it out on my father.

"Dad," I asked, "do you believe in interdigitation before marriage?"

My father did not think it was funny at all. Visibly angry, he told me never to repeat my little joke again. Having learned what "interdigitation" meant, I still hadn't realized that the joke was in the innuendo—which had gone completely over my head. "Interdigitation," of course, means holding hands.

> **" I'd like to go back and rediscover the 'before kids' me. "**
>
> —*Mother of four*

Years later, in one of my ninth months of pregnancy, when holding hands was about the most romantic thing Bub and I could do, I remember thinking, "Yes, I even believe in interdigitation—*after* marriage."

> " **I'm happy. I think maybe it's me. . . . Do I need a psychiatrist?** "
>
> —*Mother of two*

Children can kill romance.

➤ You are always busy.

➤ You are tired.

➤ You never have time alone . . . or alone with each other.

➤ You are constantly interrupted.

➤ You can start to resent each other for not doing a fair share of the chores.

➤ You're beginning to forget what you ever saw in your partner.

➤ You may be worried about money, kids, commitments or even your job.

 Other Mothers' Voices

The Real Truth About Motherhood . . . Some of the Time

Nowadays, saying happy things is practically considered rude. Complain, and the world rushes to validate you.

When my husband, Jim, comes home at night after his twelve-hour workday, my two-and-a-half-year-old daughter and I compete for his last conscious hours like cats scrapping over a dying bird. Tonight, I waited with ebbing good humor while Elizabeth commanded Jim to name all the kids in her nursery school photo over and over again. Finally, she was satisfied. She put the picture down and said, pleasantly, "Now, me and Daddy dance."

"No fair, Liz," I cried and stomped my foot (seriously). "I waited while you talked to Daddy, and now it's my turn."

I've been married to Jim for almost eight years. I'm crazy about him. And, exasperations set aside, we're both completely crazy about our kids. On weekend mornings, Elizabeth and our ten-month-old son inevitably join us in bed. We give them bus rides and train rides and get rewarded with lots of rich baby chuckling and we think: Isn't this the greatest or what?

But just being a couple was heaven, too.   —*Anonymous*

> **" Happiness consists of living each day as if it were the first day of your honeymoon and the last day of your vacation. "**
>
> —*Anonymous*

Trying to keep romance alive when you have children is not impossible, but it can become very difficult. You both agree to put the children first and spend as much time as possible with them. Besides, you are too tired to do anything once they are asleep. You tell yourself that someday soon—when the children are older, when your ship comes in, when you can afford a babysitter or the expensive restaurants in town— you will return to your B.C. (Before Children) romancing.

Humor helps, but it isn't enough. Marriage, like children, was never meant to be simply endured. Romance feeds the heart. It can turn a casserole into a banquet. It is an essential ingredient in a strong marriage.

Go on a date! According to *Webster's Dictionary,* a date is "an appointment for a specified time; esp, a social engagement between two persons of opposite sex." A date is not a dinner party for eight. Nor is it a church supper for one hundred. It is an engagement between *two* people—even if they are husband and wife. The very word "date" makes whatever you are planning special.

Problem: role reversal after marriage.

Something strange happens to married couples—liberated and unliberated alike—after their weddings and certainly after the birth of their children. Before marriage, it is often the man who asks a woman out, picks (or at least suggests) what they might do and makes the practical arrangements. After marriage, a wife seems automatically to assume responsibility for their social life. This, for many women, can mean the pits. After making certain a babysitter is in place, choosing a restaurant or movie, feeding, bathing and putting kids to bed, then taking care of herself and perhaps even suggesting appropriate clothes for her husband, many a woman simply winds down and wonders: Why go out?

> **Something deeply mysterious and profound . . . lying at the very heart of relationship . . . keeps a marriage moving, changing and shifting.**
>
> —*Thomas Moore*

Solution: One couple in a Mothers Matter group decided to choose a weeknight for their regular date. Budgeting the time and the money took real dedication.

To add a little to their special arrangement, they decided to alternate turns taking responsibility for the date. Getting the sitter, funding the fun and choosing the activity were the planner's sole responsibility for the week. Sometimes it would be a surprise. Sometimes he would pick a hockey game when she might have preferred a movie. Yet, the following week, it was her turn to take charge. What they discovered was that it kept the mystery in their relationship alive. Their romantic competition encouraged creativity and was part of the fun.

> **" I give him sex coupons for the chores he hates to do."**
>
> —*Happy mother of two*

Other Mothers' Voices

A Living Room Romance

A group of young mothers in central New Jersey were sharing secrets in one Mothers Matter session. How did they manage to keep romance alive in marriage? I had asked. A young woman I would soon come to admire began her story.

"We had just moved into a new town, and my husband was starting his own business," she explained. Thirteen women quieted down and listened intently. The speaker was calm, pulled-together emotionally, sure of herself. She continued, "I remember that we had no money to spare, not a cent! Actually, we were about eleven dollars short each month, and I was always robbing Peter to pay Paul, as they say. Juggling bills and making do had become a real grind.

"One night, after I had finished cleaning up the dishes and putting the kids to bed, I sat down next to my husband, Bill, and asked him what he was watching on TV. 'It's just junk,' he admitted, 'but I'm waiting for the next show.'

> **" People who postpone happiness are like children who try chasing rainbows in an effort to find the pot of gold at the rainbow's end. . . . Your life will never be fulfilled until you are happy here and now. "**
>
> —*Ken Keyes, Jr.*

"The next program came on, and it was no better than the junk he had been glued to, so I got up to put the last load of laundry into the dryer, and Bill left to walk the dog. When I got back upstairs, he was already in bed and asleep. We hadn't even kissed goodnight.

"I worried about *us* all the next day. Our marriage was going flat. Then I talked to Bill about my fears and my plan. I had checked the *TV Guide*, and on Tuesday nights there was nothing worth watching. 'From now on,' I told Bill, 'Tuesday night will be our date night.'

" 'Aw, c'mon,' he said to me. 'We don't have a dime to spare. We can't afford to date now. It won't always be like this,' he said to me. 'Just be patient, sweetheart.'

"I wasn't about to give up on my idea that easily," she told the Mothers Matter group. Everyone was listening closely. "The following Tuesday night, when I had finished my usual routine, I went in and turned off our television in the family room.

" 'Come into the living room, honey,' I said to Bill. 'What's up?' he asked. I had lit candles on the coffee table and put out beer and snacks for us. Then I said, 'If we had money we would probably go out, have a drink and talk to each other. Since we can't do that, we'll have our date right here. Now tell me, how was your day?'

"Bill moaned. He wasn't happy with my plan. 'C'mon, hon,' he said. 'I'm really beat, and I don't want to talk. If you want to talk, go right ahead. I'll listen.'

"Our Tuesday night living-room dates were tough at first. Getting Bill to talk to me was like pulling teeth, but I persevered, and after a couple of weeks of pouring on the charm and setting the tone, I knew my plan was working. We both talked. We both listened. That was three years ago, and Tuesday nights are still our special time. Only emergencies can interfere. We even have sex—in the middle of the week!"

Kay Remembers . . .

The Joy of Sex

I received a copy of *The Joy of Cooking* as a shower present before my wedding back in 1950. Both Bub and I might have liked it better if *The Joy of Sex* had been in print. I had absolutely no sex education. My mother had none either. "If you have any questions about S-E-X, just ask your father," she said to me.

When we returned home from our honeymoon, my mother came into my room, closed the door behind her, and in a lowered voice, said, "I have something to tell you."

Before she could say anything else, I said, "Mom, I think I've figured it out."

> **❝ I was depressed, and they told me to go out and get a new dress . . . for what?❞**
>
> —*New mother (in need of romance)*

"No," she said. "I don't think you know this. Never make love twice in one night. That's how twins are born."

Can you just imagine what my mother thought of the mother of quintuplets?

Just before the delivery date of our first child, I asked my mom, "What is labor like?"

She replied, "It's about eighteen hours, and you behave yourself." You see, my father was on the staff at the hospital where JoEllen would be born.

Today, not only is there sex education, but natural childbirth classes are also available. The conspiracy of silence about labor has been virtually eliminated. Unfortunately, the reality of parenting still comes as such a shock to new parents. You may not feel comfortable sharing your miserable moments. Perhaps you think that honest talk about the hard parts of parenting will make you appear to be less than loving or less than capable. A conspiracy of silence about the difficult aspects of parenting is still very much intact.

I truly believe that, in order to be better prepared, we need to share our feelings, our ideas, our successes and our failures with other parents. When you are able to increase your enjoyment as a parent to the grandest level, you may be able to discover that the sexual fulfillment that brought you to parenting in the first place is not the ultimate pleasure. **As we discovered, the climax is only the beginning.**

> " **If you ever find happiness by hunting for it, you will find it, as the old woman did her lost spectacles, safe on her own nose all the time.** "
>
> —*Josh Billings*

W

WILLIS FAMILY SNAPSHOT

My youngest brother, Danny, once asked if he could please buy one of those miniature bottles of milk. He meant a quart! He had never seen anything but gallon bottles of milk!

I don't ever remember being bored growing up in my family of ten children. There was always something going on. To this day, our sorrows are halved and our joys are doubled through sharing the stuff of life.

—Kim

At the end of Mothers Matter session number two, after discussing some of the best books for parents, Kay asks the mothers—fourteen of us—"What comes to mind when I ask you to recall your happiest childhood memory?" She has asked this question thousands of times of both mothers and fathers, and tells me, "I am always blown away by the simplicity of the joyful memories."

The room at St. Anne's Church in Fair Lawn, New Jersey, grows quiet. It's not often that mothers like ourselves reflect. We are just too busy. Yet in the very act of remembering, we come to realize what it is we are now doing for our children. Then we can see the big picture Kay is often drawing.

"You have the ability to create the happy memories your children will draw on forever," she insists. This is critical. To have happy memories from childhood is to have an emotional bank account filled with joy and strength.

16. Happy Parents . . .
Make Happy Memories

Two nights before Bub died, all ten of our children assembled around his bed. We were at home, a decision I made because there is no way ten people can get into a hospital room at one time. I had thought, "If there is one thing this man will want, it'll be his children." In a hospital room, we would have been forced to say, "You two go in, you two go out."

Jerry, the last to arrive, had just taken his final senior exam and was to graduate from Cook College of Rutgers University the following week. (We knew his dad would never

> **" Our life is good now, and I just want to remember that I made it happen. "**
>
> —*Mother of three*

die in the middle of exams.) Though the end was near, Bub could still hear us, and he acknowledged that fact. We were facing the most dreaded and horrendous thing ever to happen to our family.

That night, we drew strength from our happy memories. All of our children took turns recalling happy times spent with their father—memories they shared as well as deeply personal experiences with their dad. Emotions ran high. I stood at Bub's bedside and listened. . . .

➤ "Do you know what I remember, Daddy . . ."

➤ "Dad, do you remember when . . ."

➤ "I'll never forget the time . . ."

Christmases, holidays, birthdays, vacations, dinner table discussions, the highs and lows of our family lives together poured out. Even "my first car accident, when Daddy showed up and just hugged me" was fondly recalled. These young people didn't just stand around sorrowfully. They laughed and expressed a profound gratitude for his life. We even played some of his favorite music: fight songs from the football games he always loved as well as hymns he once sang in church. Everybody had time, time to remember and time to say good-bye. Their beloved father died thirty-six hours later.

> " **Never fear spoiling children by making them too happy. Happiness is the atmosphere in which all good affections grow.** "
>
> —*Ann Eliza Bray*

Even now, so many years after his death, Bub's presence at each of our special occasions is keenly felt because of these happy memories.

In the past twenty years, I've asked the happy memory question of both mothers and fathers thousands of times. Only once has a parent recalled receiving a material possession as a happy childhood memory. A mother recalled the day she received a piano. (I guess if I'd gotten a piano, I'd remember that too.)

The memories adults hang on to from childhood are sincere yet special gifts of caring, love, attention and time. I'm always blown away by the simplicity of the occasions. Looking back on their lives and for those significant encounters, people remember feelings—not fancy gift-wrapped boxes or elaborately planned experiences. When I consider all the energy and money we parents spend on "wow" presents, "quality" times or programmed vacations, trying to create special moments for kids, I never cease to be amazed by how insignificant such financial sacrifices become in our memory banks.

If I had kept a record, I suspect that answers would fall mostly into three categories. Two tie for first place: holidays and family vacations. Neither surprises me, yet holidays aren't memorable because of the piles of presents. It's because everyone is trying so hard to create a special happy atmosphere. Vacations, too, rank high—not because of where families traveled or exactly what they did—but because dads are usually around and moms have more time for fun. Phone calls, outside interruptions and demands are few. Meetings are missing, and playmates are back home.

> **" I remember my mother's rocking chair and sitting at her feet while she cared for the baby but talked to me."**
>
> *—Mother of two*

W

WILLIS FAMILY SNAPSHOT

We always headed to the mecca of all toy stores, F.A.O. Schwarz, on our holiday New York trips. We would get lost in the dizzying array of merchandising and incredible playthings. I would climb to the second floor, only to glide back down via the huge slide. We spent what seemed like hours—actually it *was* hours—before venturing back out on Fifth Avenue.

Walking back to Port Authority Bus Terminal to find our way to the platform, we would ask Mom, "How can there be a Santa Claus on every other corner and in every department store?" She'd say, "Well, Santa can't be everywhere, can he? He needs special people to be his helpers so everyone can get a chance to see him!" Sterling logic, I had to admit.

Soon the bus ride would be over, and we were deposited on our corner in Rutherford. As we walked up our street, I would enjoy the view of the darkened street—only subtly illuminated by our neighbors' electric tribute to the spirit of Christmas. Ah yes, the spirit of Christmas. No one else could have given a gift so special as a home to cherish: a neighborhood I was proud to call my own, a city that I could share with millions of other joy-seekers, plus a family so dear to my heart that I dare not think of being anywhere else at Christmastime. This was the greatest gift of all.

—*Dan*

It's funny how often car trips are recalled as happy memories. Of course many parents dread the enforced togetherness and the inevitable squabbling:

➤ "I get a window seat."

➤ "She's making faces at me."

➤ "He touched my leg."

➤ "This is my side, not yours."

➤ "Are we there, yet?"

Still, those hours spent traveling (and not necessarily where you were going) in the backseat build a family connection not easily forgotten.

In third place, however, is the happy memory that always begins with: "My mom and I . . ." or "My dad and I . . ." or "My grandmother and I . . ." or even "My teacher and I. . . ." I love this kind the most. When an adult chooses to share a part of ordinary, everyday life with a child, this time becomes precious—an occasion to be cherished forever.

Memories Are Made of This

Being a Princess. "My father used to call me Princess," one mother recalled. "I was the only girl in a family of four children. When my dad came home from work, he would always say, 'Come with me, Princess. Let's go buy the newspaper.' We would walk two blocks to the store. I can't even remember how old I was when our ritual began. I can recall that I had to reach up to hold his hand, and sometimes on the trip home, he would put me on his shoulders, so I must have been really young. We walked together to buy the paper until I was fourteen or fifteen years old, when my social schedule interfered.

> " **My grandfather played grocery store with me.** "
> —*Mother of two*

Holding hands with my dad . . . that's my happiest memory. To this day, I can talk about anything with my father. That was our special time, nobody else but Daddy and me."

Delivering milk. Her father was a milkman in the Bronx, and they lived above a store right there in New York City. She told her story to a Mothers Matter group that had gathered for the evening in her own palatial home. "On Saturdays," she recalled, "my father would take me along on his milk route. Back in those days, milk was delivered in bottles, and he would have to start very, very early in the morning right there at the barn. My father would make his pickup of fresh milk at the barn and then circle back to pick me up about 5:00 A.M. He would overturn one of the metal milk crates and put a folded blanket on top of it. I'd sit up on that milk crate in winter and in summer and ride with Daddy. When we finished the route, we always stopped for chocolate milk and a donut. That was our Saturday morning."

> **"The greatest possession you have is the 24 hours right in front of you."**
>
> —*God's Little Devotional Handbook*

The big hill. A big, jovial guy came up to me after one of the fathers' sessions. "I don't know whether to include this as a happy memory. I feel a little stupid. Yet it's the one thing that comes to my mind. I feel happy when I recall it."

"Go ahead," I said, "tell me."

"Well, every afternoon when my father was about to leave work and head for home, he would call my mother to say that he was on his way. My mother would then call to me that Daddy was coming. We lived at the bottom of a very steep hill—at least I thought it was steep. I would run to the top, leaving whatever game or friend I might have been involved

with. I would just run up that hill, stand at the top on the corner and wait for my father. When he arrived, he would pull the car over and open the door, and I'd hop in. He'd lean over, tousle my hair and say, 'How are you doin', son?'
Then we'd ride down the hill together. That ride together must have been over in seconds, but I certainly wouldn't have missed the experience for anything else in the world."

> " Joy is not in things, it is in us."
> —*Benjamin Franklin*

Shopping excursions. "My mother and I would always go shopping together," one mother remembered. "She would ask my opinion if she had been trying to decide which dress to buy. I felt so grown up, and afterward we almost always stopped for a lemonade. I don't really remember what either of us bought. I just remember the time together."

Baking with grandmother. "My grandmother was a great baker," someone recalled. "She probably had more time than my mother, who only baked at holiday times, but I remember how my grandmother would pull a chair up to the table so I could stand to help her. She gave me my own little ball of dough and let me play with it. I would stretch, press, roll and probably toughen my dough to an inedible consistency, but both of us were making pies. When the two pies—one big and one little—were out of the oven, she would always show everyone what I had made. I was so proud. It wasn't until years later that I discovered that she always threw away my dirty dough and made a tiny piecrust from scratch just for me."

New York City. My mother was a native Irish New Yorker. My fondest memories are of our trips into the big city from

New Jersey. We didn't have local shopping malls back then, and there was still only one Macy's and one Saks Fifth Avenue. They were in New York City. We had such fun together, and I enjoyed her company tremendously. She had two rules for our trips: one, we always went to say a prayer of thanksgiving at St. Patrick's Cathedral, and two, we always brought a new tie home for my father. Mom knew her way around the city and tried to teach me her tricks. "Before you give money to any nun with a collection basket, check out the shoes. If she is wearing men's shoes, it's not really a nun."

> " **My dad took me inside a wave.** "
> —*Mother of three*

Kay Remembers . . .

A Heavenly Halloween

I had never heard of the Hotel Ponchartrain in Detroit, but there I was, on October 31, 1984, being escorted to my room. Prettier than I had expected and definitely designed for a woman, the room was done in pale shades of aqua. The bellhop pointed out that the expansive view overlooked Canada on the opposite shore and suggested I leave the draperies open as I fell asleep so I could enjoy the lights. The last motel I had stayed in with my husband was a Motel 6 on our way to Notre Dame—an economy stop—with a phone booth outside our door. This room had three phones (in the bathroom, next to the bed and beside the sofa). Besides the king-size bed, there was an armoire (where I later discovered the TV), two wing chairs, the sofa, a coffee table and a desk. I was tempted to phone home and send for several relatives to share the fun. I couldn't recall ever staying in a hotel room alone, and the only traveling I'd done was my frequent trips to Florida to visit my aging parents.

After unpacking, I went down to the dining room to join Phil, the young publicist who was my traveling companion for my new career as a spokesperson. I was on tour for Fisher-Price Toys and simply loving it. As I walked into the dining room, I noticed a young woman with long blond hair playing the harp. I felt like I had died and gone to heaven!

I was being paid to travel and to be interviewed for television, radio and newspapers about my thoughts on the value of play and toys. Not only could I order whatever I wanted from the menu, but there were no cooking, no dishes and no cleanup to consider. I had just had a great day being on two TV broadcasts as well as a radio show, and my lunchtime had been spent with a newspaper columnist who loved what I had to say. No one interrupted me, and not once during my sumptuous dinner did I have to cut anybody's meat.

> **" I remember always going to my friend's house because mine wasn't any fun. "**
> —*Mother of two*

In the elevator, going back up to my room later, the first pangs of homesickness hit me. It was Halloween, the first Halloween since my marriage that I wasn't home in Rutherford. Halloween has always been one of my favorite celebrations. My first grandchild, Jamie, was six at the time, and I hated missing his excited reports about trick-or-treating.

I was barely back in my room when there was a knock on my door. When I opened it, a maid stood holding a miniature shopping bag bearing the hotel's seal. "Would you like a mint?" she asked. Without thinking (obviously), I exclaimed, "I can't believe a hotel this sophisticated is handing out Halloween candy. How nice!" She hesitated for a second and then started to laugh. "For a minute I thought you were serious," she said.

It wasn't until the next night, when I returned to my room and found my bed turned down and a mint on my pillow (the hotel's nightly routine), that I was smart enough to be embarrassed.

"Mother of ten, take the straw out of your hair," I said to myself. "This is the 'other' world, and you have found it."

I'm still finding it. Drawing strength from great memories is wonderful, of course. But creating happy memories is still a lot of fun.

To share your ideas with

Mothers Matter

write to Kay Willis and Maryann B. Brinley at:
Mothers Matter
P.O. Box 1556
Rutherford, New Jersey 07070